TOO QUIRKY, TOO QUICK, 2E

TOO QUIRKY, TOO QUICK, 2E
TWICE-EXCEPTIONAL GIFTED STUDENTS

A HANDBOOK FOR TEACHERS
EDITED BY DR SUSAN NIKAKIS AND RHIANNON LOWREY

Published in 2025 by Amba Press, Melbourne, Australia
www.ambapress.com.au

© 2025 selection and editorial matter, Susan Nikakis and Rhiannon Lowrey; individual chapters, the contributors

All rights reserved. No part of this book may be reproduced or transmitted in any form or by any means, electronic or mechanical, including photocopying, recording or by any information storage and retrieval system, without prior permission in writing from the publisher.

Cover design: Tess McCabe
Internal design: Amba Press

ISBN: 9781923215689 (pbk)
ISBN: 9781923215696 (ebk)

A catalogue record for this book is available from the National Library of Australia.

Contents

Acknowledgements		vii
About the Editors		ix
About the Contributors		xi

Introduction: *Dr Susan Nikakis* — 1

Chapter 1 — Double Trouble: Unmasking Twice Exceptionality
Rhiannon Lowrey — 3

Chapter 2 — Unicorn Hunting: Identifying Twice-Exceptional Gems
Dr Susan Nikakis and Rhiannon Lowrey — 17

Chapter 3 — IEPs, PLP's and ILPs: More Than Alphabet Soup
Dr Susan Nikakis — 39

Chapter 4 — Curriculum Remix: Navigating 2e Learning Landscapes
Dr Christine Ireland — 59

Chapter 5 — Gifted Yet Hindered – Explaining Impaired Cognitive Functions
Catherine Cross — 79

Chapter 6 — Emotions R Us: Triumph Tempered by Fear and Failure
Nina Thomas — 99

Chapter 7 — Brilliant Brains
Nina Thomas — 121

Chapter 8 — Tag Team Champions: Educator-Family Dream Team
Geraldine Nicholas — 133

Chapter 9 — Thinking Differently is His Superpower:
CASE STUDY Billy
Mark Smith — 141

Chapter 10	Unravelling the 'ced ch'2e' Riddle: Quirky Homeschooling Adventures	
	Rhiannon Lowrey	153
Chapter 11	Celebrating 2e Success Stories: Role Models to Roll After	
	Rhiannon Lowrey	161
Chapter 12	Resources for 2e Success	
	Dr Susan Nikakis	173
Chapter 13	The Continuum of Empowerment: Sustaining 2e Support	
	Dr Christine Ireland	187
Chapter 14	Continuing the Adventure: A Future of 2e Excellence	
	Rhiannon Lowrey	197

Acknowledgements

Dr Susan Nikakis

Reflecting on my professional journey, I am grateful for the diverse roles and experiences that have shaped my commitment to gifted education. Serving as Vice President of the Victorian Association for Gifted and Talented Children (VAGTC) has allowed me to collaborate with passionate advocates dedicated to nurturing gifted potential. My current position with Melbourne Archdiocese Catholic Schools (MACS) enables me to recommend pedagogical improvements tailored to gifted students, ensuring their unique needs are met within our educational system.

Supervising doctoral students at the University of Melbourne has been particularly rewarding, as it allows me to mentor emerging scholars in the field. Additionally, authoring and editing four books focused on gifted education has provided me with the opportunity to share insights and strategies with a broader audience. Presenting papers and delivering keynote addresses at both international and national conferences have further enriched my understanding and advocacy for gifted learners.

Enhancing the quality of teaching has always been a cornerstone principle of Amba Press, and I am profoundly grateful to see this vision reflected in our work. The commitment to elevating professional practice and fostering a culture of inclusion is at the very heart of this publication. I am especially thrilled and deeply thankful to Alicia Cohen, whose unwavering belief in the power of education and dedication to this mission once again led her to publish our book.

This book is more than a resource; it is a testament to what is possible when educators are empowered with the tools, knowledge, and mindset to truly make a difference. I firmly believe that addressing the learning needs of gifted students is a matter of justice, and I am committed to continuing this vital work.

Rhiannon Lowrey

This book is dedicated to those who have walked beside me, those who have come before, and those who continue to navigate a world that often doesn't quite fit. It is a tribute to anyone who has ever felt like a round peg in a square world – the unicorns among us, whose uniqueness is their greatest gift. To the neurodivergent community, this book is for you.

As a neurodivergent teacher, I have often heard members of this beautiful and vibrant community described as "too" – too loud, too quiet, too weird, too unsettled, too fast at completing tasks. Always "too much." Over time, I've come to understand that what is labelled as "too much" is often exactly what the world needs.

I am deeply grateful to Dr Susan Nikakis, without whom this book would not have come to life. Dr Nikakis is a champion, cheerleader, and tireless advocate for every gifted child and adult she encounters. Her passion for education, her unwavering dedication to the neurodivergent community, and her belief in the power of inclusion have inspired and guided me throughout this journey. She has been both a mentor and a partner in this endeavour, and I am honoured to know her and call her my friend.

I would also like to thank the co-contributors and experts who have enriched these pages with their knowledge and insights. Their expertise has brought depth and nuance to this book. I would also like to express my gratitude to Amba Press and Alicia Cohen, who believed in this project and dared to disrupt the norms of educational publishing to amplify voices that deserve to be heard.

Finally, to my husband, children, and family, you are my rock, my light, and my greatest champions. You have been my glimpse into neurotypical understanding, my partners in laughter, and my comfort during tears. Without your love, support, and unwavering belief in me, this book would not exist. You have my deepest gratitude.

About the Editors

Dr Susan Nikakis

Dr Susan Nikakis currently serves as a Senior Gifted Education Officer at Melbourne Archdiocese Catholic Schools (MACS), where she develops and implements pedagogical improvements for gifted education. With more than 30 years' experience in education, she has held various leadership positions, including Deputy Principal, across six secondary schools, consistently championing the rights of all students to receive appropriate and thoughtful education.

Throughout her career, Dr Nikakis has made significant contributions to gifted education through her roles as Director of the Australian Association for the Education of Gifted and Talented Students and current Vice-President of the Victorian Association for Gifted and Talented Children. She regularly delivers keynote addresses at national and international conferences, focusing on gifted student education and fostering rigorous discussion in the field.

As an accomplished author and editor, Dr Nikakis has authored numerous books and articles on gifted education. Her publications reflect her ongoing commitment to advancing educational practices for gifted learners while modelling best practices for the next generation of educators.

Rhiannon Lowrey

Rhiannon Lowrey is a passionate educator, advocate, and leader in the field of gifted and twice-exceptional (2e) education. She currently serves as a Board Member of the Australian Association for the Education of the Gifted and Talented (AAEGT). She is the National Gifted Awareness Week Director, where she plays a key role in national advocacy and awareness initiatives. Rhiannon is also the High Potential and Gifted Leader at her school, where she designs and implements programs that support the diverse needs of gifted and 2e learners.

With over 15 years of experience across primary, secondary, and tertiary education, Rhiannon has developed expertise in curriculum differentiation, inclusive pedagogies, and student-centred learning. Her passion for gifted education is deeply personal, as she has lived experience as a twice-exceptional individual, giving her a unique perspective on both the challenges and strengths of neurodiverse learners.

This is Rhiannon's first book, and she hopes to continue to write and speak on inclusive education in the future, advocating for systemic change, better teacher training, and increased support for high-potential and twice-exceptional students. She believes that every learner deserves an environment where their strengths are celebrated and their challenges are supported. Rhiannon is committed to fostering a more inclusive, responsive, and empowering education system where all students, particularly those who are gifted and 2e, can thrive.

About the Contributors

Catherine Cross

Catherine Cross is a Gifted and Talented leader and educator, who coordinates and teaches, the gifted and twice-exceptional program in an independent College in Melbourne. With over 30 years of teaching experience and holding three degrees in education, including a Master's in Gifted and Talented Education, she has specialised expertise in tailoring gifted learning programs to incorporate social-emotional strategies, critical and creative thinking, higher-order thinking, and rich inquiry learning for high ability students. As a twice-exceptional person herself, she furthered her studies in counselling and neurodivergence to enhance her ability to cater for the psychosocial wellbeing of her students and further endeavoured to become a Gifted Education Consultant.

Dr Christine Ireland

Christine Ireland is an ex-president of the Victorian and Australian Associations for Gifted Education. She lectured in Victorian universities, co-ordinated primary and secondary schools' gifted education, has completed a doctorate of gifted education and has presented over twenty national and international papers for gifted education events, books and magazines. In addition to co-ordinating gifted education programs, Christine has taught English, science, history and geography for over 20 years.

Geraldine Nicholas

Geraldine Nicholas is the Professional Learning Coordinator for Tournament of Minds. This program has been around for 35 years and continues to enchant and enthral students across all sectors and year levels. Geraldine has also worked in several schools across both primary and secondary years as gifted coordinator teaching within the gifted program. She has experience in developing and reviewing gifted programs as well as working with the learning services faculty at her present school. She has an ongoing commitment to meeting the needs of gifted and talented students.

Mark Smith

Mark Smith is an innovative educator with more than 30 years' experience in the Victorian education system across all sectors. He holds a Master of Education, Gifted and Talented Education acquired via course work and research at Monash University. Mark is best known for his work in gifted and talented education where he has created and implemented large multi-faceted school wide programs at some of Melbourne's largest independent schools. He is passionate about best practice teaching and learning approaches and has facilitated outstanding results with students of all ages, many gifted, using mentoring as a means of cultivating student engagement, agency, and self-efficacy. He is the author or *Mentoring for Talent*, another Amba Press publication, and since the end of 2022, he has been working full-time as an Educational Consultant.

Nina Thomas

Nina Thomas is a psychotherapist whose career has spanned multiple fields, each deepening her understanding of human development, learning, and wellbeing. With a professional journey that has taken her through education, psychology, advocacy, and various other industries, she has witnessed firsthand the unique challenges faced by gifted and twice-exceptional (2e) individuals. These experiences have reinforced her commitment to helping neurodivergent individuals develop not only their cognitive strengths but also their emotional resilience, self-advocacy, and sense of identity. Nina integrates her wealth of experience into her clinical work, providing individualised support to clients seeking to better understand themselves and their unique ways of thinking, learning, and feeling.

Introduction

Dr Susan Nikakis

"The things that make me different are the things that make me."
Winnie the Pooh

Students who are both gifted and have a disability are often overlooked. It's a fact, because it's proven that individuals can be simultaneously very intelligent and have something else; a disability or difference like ADHD, autism, dyslexia, or anxiety that can work against the expression of their abilities (MacEachron, 2019).

Twice-exceptionality is both a fact and a movement. And the movement is finally taking off!

Twice-exceptional learners are students who demonstrate the potential for high achievement or creative productivity in one or more domains such as math, science, technology, the social arts, the visual, spatial, or performing arts or other areas of human productivity AND who manifest one or more disabilities as defined by federal or state eligibility criteria. These disabilities include specific learning disabilities; speech and language disorders; emotional/behavioural disorders; physical disabilities; autism spectrum disorders (ASD); or other health impairments, such as attention deficit hyperactivity disorder (ADHD). These disabilities and high abilities combine to produce a unique population of students who may fail to demonstrate either high academic performance or specific disabilities. Their gifts may mask their disabilities, and their disabilities may mask their gifts (Reis et al., 2014).

A meeting of minds

I first encountered Rhiannon during a workshop for teachers that I was facilitating, and from the very beginning, her insights and experiences struck a profound chord with me. It was clear that she approached education with a depth of understanding and empathy that few possess, and her passion for supporting twice-exceptional (2e) students was both inspiring and contagious. As we engaged in conversations, I quickly recognised her as a kindred spirit, someone who not only shared my dedication to these remarkable learners but also brought her own invaluable perspectives and expertise to the table.

Through our conversations, Rhiannon has significantly enriched my understanding of the complex and nuanced world of 2e students, opening my eyes to new approaches and possibilities that continue to shape my work in gifted education. Our joint enthusiasm for this crucial area of giftedness had us move from respected colleague to admired and appreciated friends.

Why this book?

What motivated the idea for an Australian (sorry very Victorian biased) book on twice exceptional was the dearth of local resources. It is bad enough that many teachers think that gifted students can flourish on their own, but should they have dyscalculia or ADHD then forget it! Often teachers will only ever see the disability. We began to see a gaping hole in books for teachers on practical ways of facilitating learning.

This book is written by educators for educators and includes:

- An overview and definitions
- Personal stories, examples and case studies
- Suggested articles, books, blog posts, podcasts and videos
- Detailed lists of practical suggestions for your classroom

These suggestions do not all need to be used all of the time, but instead provide a menu of options for your consideration. Try strategies and see what works for your classroom. We believe that you will find that it is not only 2e students who benefit from the strategies and ideas in this model; we do not want our 2e students to experience a slow momentum for interventions.

As Silverman (1993) suggests, "the cognitive complexity and certain personality traits of the gifted create unique experiences and awareness that separate them from others. A central feature of the gifted experience is their moral sensitivity, which is essential to the welfare of the entire society."

CHAPTER I

Double Trouble: Unmasking Twice Exceptionality

Rhiannon Lowrey

In the world of education, where each student brings a unique set of challenges and talents, some students seem to defy categorisation altogether. These are the twice exceptional or 2e, the dynamic individuals who possess both exceptional gifts in a variety of classifications and a neurodiversity such as a diagnosed learning difficulty, such as ADHD, ASD, dyslexia, specific learning difficulty (SLD). Children and adults that might not fit the conventional moulds we have become accustomed to, that stereotype both individual groups. They embody asynchronous learners (Silverman, 1993).

In this chapter, we're going to peel back the layers of complexity surrounding twice exceptionality (2e) and explore what it truly means for academic professionals. Think of it as unmasking a superhero – a student who doesn't just fit the 'gifted' or 'special needs' label, but rather wears a cape woven from both.

Understanding the dual identity

Let's start by shattering the myth that giftedness and learning differences are mutually exclusive. In fact, 2e students represent the intersection of these two worlds, creating an extraordinary blend of abilities and challenges. As academic professionals, it's vital to embrace this duality and recognise that these students possess unique cognitive profiles that defy standard expectations.

These students will not present as clear cut, stereotypical or cookie cutter versions of the described models. As new research comes to light it becomes easier to diagnose and identify 2e individuals. The current testing practice by educational psychologists is largely based around the deficit model, what people are unable to achieve that they should be able to for their age, these include but are not limited to the following screening tools, ASQ, (Ages and Stages Questionnaire), CSBS (Communication and Symbolic Behaviour Scales) PEDS, (Parent Evaluation and Developmental Status, MCHAT (Modified Checklist for Autism in Toddlers), STAT (Screening Tool for Autism in Toddlers and Young Children), ADOS (Autism Diagnostic Observation Schedule). All these tests are tools for tracking norms of behaviours, there is no medical test for the diagnosis of ASD, ADHD or any other specific learning disabilities. If testing for learning difficulties is hard then testing for giftedness could be seen as almost impossible.

There are similar metrics used to identify giftedness the GSAM (Gifted Student Ability Metric), the Cognitive Abilities Test (CogAT), Comprehensive Test of Nonverbal Intelligence (CTONI-2), the Universal Nonverbal Intelligence scale (UNIT-2), Stanford-Binet 5th Edition (SB-5), Wechsler Preschool Primary Scale of Intelligence (WPPSI-IV) and Wechsler Intelligence Scale for Children (WISC-V), in addition to IQ testing. These tests are all highly respected and do give a good indication of the academic giftedness of the person, however they have their limits, they do not test for any non-academic gifted trait. They also do not test for 2e people, many students with neurodiversity such as ASD, ADHD, and language disorders find test taking to be traumatic. Perfectionism, which is a trait of many gifted students, will find themselves incapable of completing the test, or even starting without the guarantee that they will score a perfect score, self-expectation can hinder their ability to start. As we know standardised tests were designed to test standards not exceptions.

Figure 1: Perspective From the Spectrum

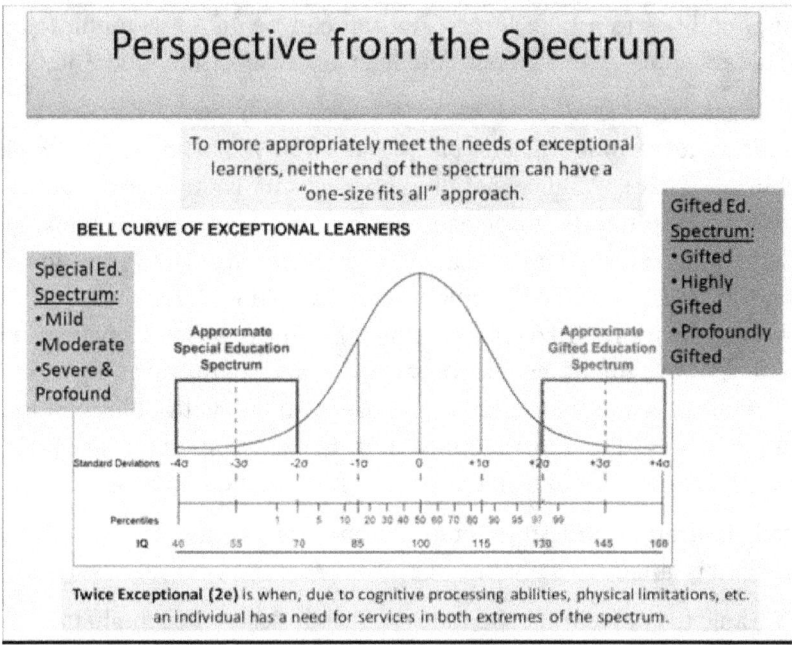

GILBERT, G. (2014, APRIL). ASYNCHRONOUS DEVELOPMENT. GILBERT GIFTED. HTTPS://GILBERTGIFTED.BLOGSPOT.COM/2014/04/ASYNCHRONOUS-DEVELOPMENT.HTML

Figure 1 shows the cell curve in which there is approximately equal groupings of students at both ends of the bell curve. Society mirrors school in that there is a greater emphasis – no one is left behind, but the equity does not extend to those who are more capable and learn faster.

Breaking down the definitions

What exactly does it mean to be twice exceptional (2e)? We will delve into the definitions, encompassing giftedness and learning disabilities, ADHD, autism, and more. We will explore the spectrum of abilities and the shades of grey that can make 2e students hard to pin down.

As outlined in the last section there are a multitude of tests that can assist with the identification of gifted students and those students with a disability.

So, what is giftedness? Is a child, bright, clever, academic, brilliant, talented, or gifted?

Many advocacy groups define giftedness as: those children are born with above average natural abilities. Talented children have developed their natural abilities to a high level. Children can be gifted in multiple areas, sports, art, music, emotional intelligence, leadership, and intellectual ability.

Advanced development is one of the signs that your child might be gifted (Robinson, 2020). You'll generally know if your child is more advanced than other children the same age. For example, some intellectually gifted children teach themselves to read at a young age, like 2–3 years old. Some physically advanced children might excel early in junior sports or physical activities, musically gifted children might be able to pick up any instrument and play, others might be able to listen to a piece of music and play by ear. Another sign is that your child might prefer to talk with older children or adults (Gross, 2011). For example, your 4-year-old might relate better to 6-year-olds or even adults better than to children their own age.

Gifted children also learn differently from other children. For example, if your child is gifted, they might:

- Be able to concentrate and focus well on tasks, or they might not.
- Be intensely curious and ask sharp questions, or they might not speak, or take time to consider their answer.
- Learn very quickly, especially in their passion and interest.
- Have an extremely good memory for facts and figures, but forget to do everyday things, might lack organisation and executive functioning.
- Be very imaginative and creative, see, hear, and feel the world differently.
- Have advanced speech, vocabulary, and topics.

Recognising the quirks and strengths

2e students often come with a parade of quirks, idiosyncrasies, and unconventional behaviours. But hidden beneath these quirks are remarkable strengths that, when harnessed, can lead to exceptional achievements. We will explore the unique cognitive abilities of 2e learners and how these talents can be nurtured to shine.

Positive psychology has recently heavily emphasised the strengths-based approach to learning, this is especially important for all students, but more importantly our neurodiverse students (Seligman, 2011). 2e students are different, they feel different in the classroom, they are smart enough to recognise that they don't 'fit' with their peers, this is often compounded by relating better to adults and older students, who have a more mature and complex understanding of the world.

The strengths based approach is just that, instead of focusing on the negative, the deficit, the dysregulation, the teacher, or educator focuses on the strength. Each student possesses their own set of unique strengths, which encompass their interests, positive attributes, special skills, and inherent abilities. These personal traits define their individuality and contribute to their overall identity.

When we acknowledge and emphasise these personal strengths, it triggers a release of dopamine response in the child, providing positive feedback that resonates throughout the nervous system (Hariri and Holmes, 2015). This 'feel-good' sensation travels through the brain and body, influencing various aspects of an individual's life. It can aid in regulating emotions, enhancing mood, influencing behaviour, facilitating effective communication, and promoting active participation. Reducing the negative impact of a person's disability. Recognising and nurturing these strengths in each student not only celebrates their individuality but also contributes to their holistic development and wellbeing.

There are as always limitations. In a class of 26–30 students educators cannot cater to all the needs of all the students all the time, however something educators can do is offer choice.

In a subject, for example in English; it could be the same task but using a different text, in line with the students' strengths. It could be the same text as the peers, but the application is different. The students could use artistic materials or media to communicate the answer if writing is problematic.

In mathematics it could be using specially designed software to gamify concepts, rather than rote learning topics. It could be taking a deep dive into a singular specific area in maths and completing a project showing depth of curiosity and understanding, trying and testing formulas and proofs, trying to develop a new formula.

In science it could be connecting with external scientists either by watching videos/listening to podcasts/asking questions and making connections like the CSIRO scientist in schools' program. It could involve testing and creating new products and combining or updating current technology to make them better.

History students can link in with archaeologists and do virtual tours of ancient dig sites that have been rendered digitally to fill in the ruins. Teachers could also make cultural connections to indigenous people in the area to gain deeper understanding of the history and culture of the land. The possibilities are endless.

Many teachers will struggle with the idea of extra workload for one student. A possible time saving strategy for a classroom teacher is giving 2e students access to present passion projects using the 3 min thesis model. To do this they must synthesise and condense all the key ideas into 3 mins, making it achievable for educators to assess the knowledge but also allows students to build new skills in knowledge synthesis, and communication strategies. This strategy will frustrate some learners as they will feel like they have more knowledge than can fit into 3 minutes. In my experience advising students that they can build new skills to demonstrate their knowledge is just as important as the knowledge. Such students will often relish in the challenge of making the video or presentation exactly 3 minutes long. Software like Apple movie editor can be used to make a movie trailer to capture shot videos and editing can assist younger students, whereas older students might like to try more professional software to develop more complex skills.

Redefining challenges

Challenges are part of every student's journey, but for 2e students, they might be doubly complex. We will dive into the unique hurdles they face – the frustration of potential unrealised, the mismatch between cognitive capabilities and emotional maturity, and the struggle to find peers who understand their world.

Academic challenges can look different for each student, students with dyslexia can struggle in subjects where reading and writing dominate. If a student is gifted in mathematics, but cannot read the question due to literacy issues, it does not diminish the student's giftedness in maths. It means that the teacher or educator needs to redefine the challenge, make video content, use tools such as c-pen (can be problematic with the speed and capacity to only read small quantities of text) to help the child navigate the difficulty and flourish in their gifting. It is harder for students with neurological diversity such as autism and ADHD, as many educators see the behaviour issues before they see the learner. They see a person that cannot sit still, fidgeting, stimming, or using sensory tools, and they view these variables as obstacles in their classroom that might prevent good learning. The strategies for self-regulation are sometimes distractions to neurotypical learners, they can also trigger other neurodiverse students with alternative sensory needs.

Many educators and academics agree 2e students should not be disadvantaged by their disability. However some disabilities, are seen as easier to accommodate than others. We as educators often feel that if we meet a sensory need for a learner the learning should just happen. A good example to help position teachers is that of a student in a wheelchair. Often we will make accommodations to allow that student to access the campus and move freely and play with other learners. We will put in specialised play equipment and change the games and activities, desks and classroom layouts to allow that student to feel as 'normal' as possible at school. We do the same thing with neurodiverse learners. We put in place, action plans, sensory spaces, quiet activities, sensory gardens etc. The biggest difference is once we put these activities in place, we feel like the learner is ready to go and we don't need to continually adjust as we have met their needs. The child with an invisible disability or neurodiversity is having to use large amounts of effort at their end to action within the accommodations. This idea is positioned by the difference between visible and invisible disability. Once we give a student a wheelchair, we don't demand that they build their own ramps. Yet with invisible disability I have sat in many support meetings where it has been explained, "but I gave them fidget time, or they can leave the room to regroup," but what they need is to make the time up at lunch. Ultimately punishing a student for taking the time they need to regulate in class time by removing them at social and play times. Research from Attwood (2023) has shown that neurodiverse students need to have access to social play.

The role of professionals

As educators, you play a crucial role in identifying, supporting, and advocating for 2e students. In this section, we will discuss the impact that academic professionals can have on the 2e experience. From recognising potential signs to tailoring instruction and fostering an inclusive classroom environment, your influence is paramount.

The role of an academic professional is to meet the learner at the point of need. With 2e students the point of need can change each subject, but also each lesson, educators need to educate all 30 students in their care, therefore accommodating the individual needs of each student can be challenging. Primary educators statistically are better at accommodating individual needs as they have more classroom time to build relationship, see patterns of behaviour, adapt, and accommodate as needed, and flex as they are not bound by the same limitations (Hattie, 2003). Primary educators still face challenges. Secondary teachers do not get the same time to build relationship before the bell goes and the student moves into the new class. The second challenge for secondary teachers is they are not aware of the students level of distress prior to them walking into the room. Therefore, they will likely not allow for any adaptions as they are driven by the need to 'get through the curriculum'. A benefit of being a secondary educator is their pedagogical content knowledge. Usually teaching in their method allows them to dig into a concept differently, to go deeper, to flex into another explanation or interpretation allowing for varied understanding as they can see the problem from multiple angles.

Other difficulties arise as students mature and the impact of their giftedness can be lessened. The learner might have been able to read at 2 or 3 years old, but the difference with other learners is significantly lessened by 16 or 17, when most students can read the same texts (Peterson and Kellison, 2021). Many students who are 2e or gifted learners, hate being labelled and identified as gifted learners, this is often due to the resulting expectations of the teacher and parents. As teenagers gifted learners have often developed deep trauma from their earlier years of education.

As teachers and educators, we need to be continually mindful that these students exist in our classes. Establishing relationships and building trust is paramount in all levels of education. Additionally I have found that my students benefit from me disclosing my diagnosis. I clearly and succinctly explain to the class how I present when overwhelmed, what I might need from them as a group of people and this usually results in 3-4 students per year coming to me in private and explaining what works for them academically and socially. Many parents have also spoken to me with tears in their eyes stating that their learner has seen hope through making connections with an adult that truly understands their struggle and sees them in their difficulty. My position is unique as I can speak from a place of knowledge and understanding. But all educators regardless of time with students can make time to set classroom expectations and explain why they are an expectation. Why is iut that we don't swing on the chair? Because it makes me see danger and makes me as the teacher feel sad thinking you could hurt yourself. It adds to my worry and stress meaning I cannot focus on the lesson well. Students are people, they like to understand and allowing transparency in rules and expectations is good for everyone.

My hope is that as you progress through this book, you begin to see the world through a lens of acceptance and not just acknowledgement. The difference is acknowledgement means you know I am there; acceptance means you are happy to have me.

Embracing the quirkiness

To truly support 2e students, we need to embrace the quirkiness that comes with their unique cognitive profiles. Let's challenge the traditional notion of what a "typical" student looks like and celebrate the diversity of minds in our classrooms. By doing so, we create a space where 2e students can thrive, and their exceptional qualities can flourish.

Asynchronous development as previously mentioned is typical development for a gifted and therefore also a 2e child (Gilbert, 2014). Twice-exceptional children often exhibit asynchronous development, a concept recognised in the field of gifted education. Asynchronous development refers to the uneven or out-of-sync progression of various developmental domains in these individuals. While 2e children may demonstrate advanced intellectual abilities and creativity, their social, emotional, or executive functioning skills may lag. Falling behind their peers. Silverman (1993) observed that asynchronous development can result in unique challenges for these learners, as their advanced cognitive abilities may be masked or overshadowed by behavioural or emotional struggles. This asynchrony underscores the importance of individualised support and understanding in addressing the complex needs of 2e children.

Stephanie Newitt (2014) outlines the difference between typical child development and asynchronous development, see Figure 2 and 3 respectively.

Figure 2: Typical Child Development

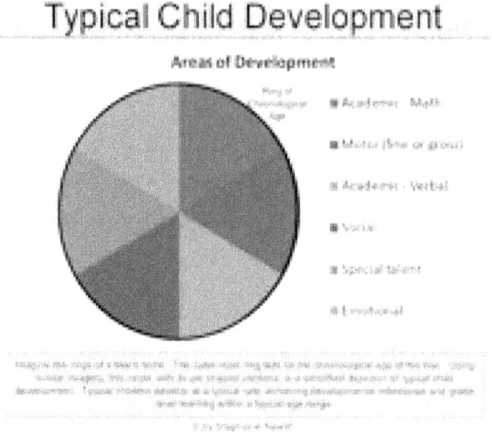

Figure 3: Asynchronous Development

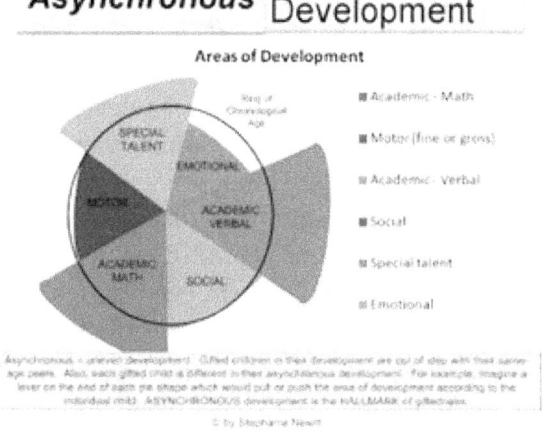

Dr Linda Silverman has stated, "... gifted children develop in an uneven manner, ... they are more complex and intense than their agemates, ... they feel out-of-sync with age peers and 'age-appropriate curriculum,' ... the internal and external discrepancies increase with IQ, and ... these differences make them extremely vulnerable."

This vulnerability can cause 2e students to mark their giftedness, to see perfectionism and create unrealistic expectations of themselves.

Kathryn's story

In my 15 years as a primary and secondary teacher, I've had the privilege of working with a diverse range of students. Among them, one young girl named Kathryn (though that's not her real name) left a lasting impression. Kathryn was nothing short of brilliant. She possessed a remarkable ability to read, a talent that emerged at a very young age, and she had a voracious appetite for books.

Our paths crossed when I had the honour of teaching Kathryn in an extension program designed for gifted students. It was immediately evident that she was in a league of her own when it came to reading. She enthusiastically participated in every academic challenge she could find. One competition, the ACER Global Challenge, focused on reading skills. Kathryn decided to take the plunge and participate.

I vividly remember the day when she received her results. The excitement in her eyes was palpable. The grade she earned placed her in the top 3% of the world in her age group for reading. It was a testament to her exceptional abilities. Kathryn was, without a doubt, an extraordinary reader.

But Kathryn's story wasn't just about academic prowess. She faced a formidable challenge – an overwhelming level of anxiety. She struggled with situational mutism; a condition that made it almost impossible for her to speak in certain situations. Amid her brilliance, she would physically freeze, unable to utter a sound.

Determined to provide Kathryn with the support she deserved, I shared her remarkable test results with her English teacher, expecting a shared sense of pride in her achievements. To my surprise, the response I received was far from what I expected. Her English teacher saw no giftedness in Kathryn's abilities and dismissed her accomplishments as mere luck. It was a disheartening moment, and I couldn't help but feel frustrated. Kathryn was unable to communicate in class, feeling misaligned with her classroom teacher her mutism would exacerbate, meaning she was unable to share her thoughts and feelings about texts. Her teacher was not able to see the knowledge as she was only looking in a traditional way.

That's when I began to delve deeper into the concept of twice exceptionality. I wanted to understand and communicate to others that Kathryn's challenges didn't negate her giftedness. However, when I tried to explain this to some colleagues, I was met with scepticism. Some believed that 2e wasn't a legitimate concept, doubting it as a possibility.

Despite these setbacks, Kathryn's experience served as a turning point in my journey as an educator. I was determined to be her advocate, to champion her success, and to remind her that her brilliance was unquestionable, regardless of others' opinions. Kathryn trusted my voice as her advocate, and I was committed to ensuring she had the opportunity to excel.

One of those opportunities came in 2023 when Kathryn was invited to conduct self-research in our extension program. Her dedication and hard work paid off as she was selected to present her findings at an international conference. It was a momentous occasion, and while she was understandably nervous, I made it my mission to be there for her every step of the way. I reminded her that her best was always good enough and that she was brilliant, no matter what anyone else thought.

As Kathryn stood proudly at the dais of a university; microphone in hand; at an international conference and presented her research, I couldn't have been prouder. Her journey from being underestimated to shining on a global stage was nothing short of inspiring. Kathryn's story is a testament to the incredible potential within 2e students, waiting to be unlocked with the right support and advocacy.

In the end, Kathryn's experience reaffirmed my belief in the importance of recognising and nurturing the unique strengths and needs of 2e learners. They may face challenges that obscure their gifts, but with the right guidance and unwavering support, they can achieve greatness. Kathryn's story is a reminder that as educators, we have the privilege and responsibility to be champions for these exceptional students. Kathryn's journey serves as a powerful reminder of the impact educators can have on 2e students. It underscores the need for understanding, patience, and advocacy to help these exceptional learners thrive. These students need the opportunity to excel, and they rely on educators like you to be their champions. Your dedication to supporting 2e learners like Kathryn is truly commendable and exemplifies the transformative power of education.

Continue this expedition into the world of 2e education, where each student is a puzzle piece that doesn't quite fit yet completes the picture in ways unimaginable. As we embark on this journey together, you'll gain insights into the minds and hearts of 2e students, equipping you with the knowledge and tools to make a lasting impact on their educational experience.

KEY TAKEAWAYS

- **Understanding twice exceptionality (2e):** Twice-exceptional individuals possess both exceptional abilities in specific areas and neurodiversity, such as ADHD, ASD, or specific learning disabilities. They challenge conventional educational stereotypes and require a nuanced approach to accommodate their asynchronous development.

- **Testing challenges and misalignments:** Current testing methods for both disabilities and giftedness often fail to capture the full scope of 2e learners' abilities. Standardised tests are designed to measure norms rather than exceptions, often disadvantaging students with neurodiversity or perfectionist tendencies.

- **Strengths-based approach:** Emphasising the strengths and passions of 2e students rather than focusing on their deficits can trigger positive responses, enhance their emotional wellbeing, and encourage active participation. Offering choices and individualised approaches within the curriculum can nurture their unique talents.

- **Complex challenges and invisible disabilities:** 2e students face academic, social, and emotional challenges, including anxiety, perfectionism, and mismatched cognitive and emotional development. The additional effort required to navigate their accommodations often goes unrecognised, and invisible disabilities are frequently misunderstood or inadequately supported.

- **Role of educators and advocacy:** Teachers play a critical role in fostering an inclusive environment, recognising 2e students' needs, and advocating for their success. Relationship-building, transparency, and adapting teaching methods can significantly impact their learning experiences, helping them thrive academically and emotionally. Kathryn's story exemplifies the transformative impact of advocacy and tailored support.

Chapter references

Attwood, T. (2023). *The complete guide to Asperger's syndrome and autism: Updated edition.* Jessica Kingsley Publishers.

Gilbert, G. (2014, April). Asynchronous Development. Gilbert Gifted. https://gilbertgifted.blogspot.com/2014/04/asynchronous-development.html

Gross, M. U. M. (2011). Exceptionally gifted children: Long-term outcomes of academic acceleration and nonacceleration. *Journal for the Education of the Gifted, 34*(4), 643-680. https://doi.org/10.1177/0162353211412917

Hariri, A. R., & Holmes, A. (2015). Finding translation in stress research. *Nature Neuroscience, 18*(10), 1347-1352. https://doi.org/10.1038/nn.4115

Hattie, J. (2003). Teachers make a difference: What is the research evidence? Paper presented at the Australian Council for Educational Research Annual Conference on Building Teacher Quality, Melbourne, Australia.

Newitt, S. (2014). Asynchronous development in gifted children. *Understanding Our Gifted, 26*(3), 18-20.

Peterson, J. S., & Kellison, I. L. (2021). Changes in giftedness across the lifespan: A systematic review. *Gifted Child Quarterly, 65*(2), 111-125. https://doi.org/10.1177/0016986220977906

Robinson, N. M. (2020). Is my child gifted? Understanding the signs and characteristics. *Parenting Today.* https://www.parentingtoday.com/article/is-my-child-gifted-understanding-the-signs-and-characteristics/

Seligman, M. E. P. (2011). *Flourish: A visionary new understanding of happiness and well-being.* Free Press.

Silverman, L. K. (1993). Asynchronous Development. Gifted Development Center. https://www.gifteddevelopment.com/Articles/asynchronous_development.pdf

CHAPTER 2

Unicorn Hunting: Identifying Twice-Exceptional Gems

Dr Susan Nikakis and Rhiannon Lowrey

Picture a classroom bustling with a diverse array of students, each with their own strengths and struggles. Amidst this vibrant mix, there are those who often elude detection – the twice-exceptional (2e) students, sometimes referred to as the "unicorns" of education. Just as the elusive mythical creature is both horse and horn, 2e students possess a blend of exceptional abilities and challenges that require a keen eye to recognise.

Dr Susan Nikakis (2023) is often quoted in her gifted education seminars as saying that when you meet a truly gifted person you will know, people with a gifting are estimated to be roughly 1 in 10 people. Meaning that in your classrooms 2-3 students will be observed as being gifted in one or more areas. Profoundly gifted people are about 1 in 1 million students, meaning you might not ever come across one in your teaching career. 2e people are even more likely to go undetected as they often have a disability that can mask their gifting or their gifting masks their disability meaning they never get the full support they need to truly thrive in education.

From data collected by schools and compiled by the Australian Bureau of Statistics on gifted students; a group that represent a unique segment of our educational landscape, with their potential to excel beyond traditional expectations. In Victoria, Australia, there are approximately 25,000 identified gifted students, constituting 10% of the student population. Zooming out to the national level, Australia boasts around 150,000 gifted students, a figure also accounting for 10% of the total student population. Globally, an estimated 25 million gifted students can be found, though they represent just around 1% of the world's population. (Australian Bureau of Statistics, 2020). These statistics underscore the importance of recognising and supporting the unique needs and talents of gifted students, both locally and on a global scale they also highlight the low rate of testing and the ineffectiveness of current methods of testing.

These numbers may seem large and globally 25 million people is a large group. It is roughly the population of Australia at time of publication. In your classrooms this number becomes more manageable, in a school of 1000 students you might identify 1–10% meaning 10–100 students. This is only true if all students globally are treated with equality. Françoys Gagné's model of identifying giftedness revolves around opportunities, therefore there is a large portion of students who are gifted but never can demonstrate it (2004, 2015). Think of learners in refugee camps or very low socio-economic environments. These learners are trying to survive, not wanting to stand out for fear of retribution for them or their families. These populations of learners are missing from our data, which changes the numbers we see in first world nations.

Why a unicorn? Are they really elusive?

As a classroom teacher with 15 years' experience, I have never once been asked to run specific testing to identify gifted or high potential students. Much of the data collected at schools reinforces the bias that education has towards those students who struggle with learning. If you look at any school across Australia you will see the inclusive education teams being made up of learning support teachers, in rare cases the 'gifted or extension teacher' may be included. Often schools have one passionate teacher pushing solo to help extend the students in his or her sphere, usually on top of a normal teaching load and with very few resources available. Private education schools which make up 36% of our compulsory academic landscape, have capacity to encourage and entice gifted and high potential students, through scholarships, status or accommodations. This means that any student who is identified as gifted is quickly offered a place at a select entry school or school that wants to profit from having educated the best of the best, focusing on the accomplishments of future alumni. If you haven't come across any gifted students in your career so far, you may be teaching in a different sector, or you may have the blessing of interacting with a unicorn.

Figure 1: Seth Perler explains twice exceptional visually

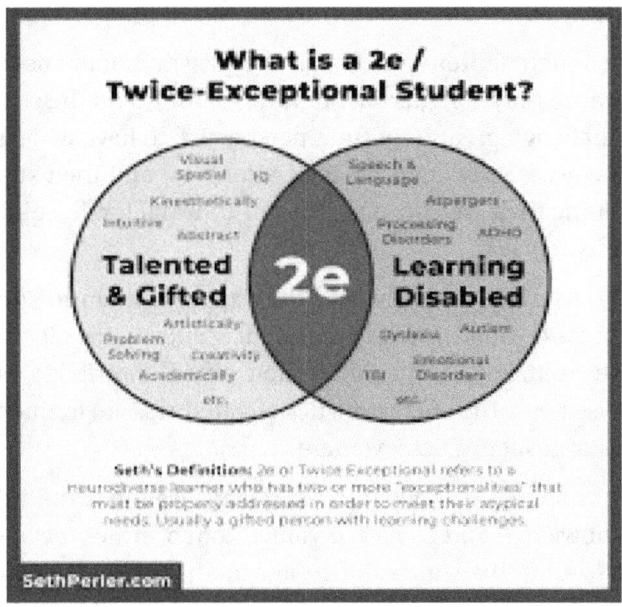

Some gifted students can also have difficulties or challenges in other areas that make their learning and success much more difficult to achieve. The reason for these labels is that a 2e child will have an exceptional gift in one area (for example, maths, reading, music, art, leadership) as well as an exceptional challenge in a different area. This challenge could be learning, social, emotional, physical or behavioural:

- A specific learning disability in areas such as reading, spelling, writing or mathematics. This could include diagnoses of dyscalculia (challenges with numbers), dysgraphia (challenges with writing) or dyslexia (challenges with reading).
- Physical disabilities that cause challenges with learning: hearing or vision impairment, or physical impairment such as quadriplegia.
- Learning challenges because of language barriers: English as an Additional Language (EAL)

- A neurodivergent diagnosis: attention deficit hyperactivity disorder, autism spectrum. Neurodiversity refers to the fact that brain differences are normal and that people with such differences can experience and interpret the world in unique ways.
- A diagnosed mental health concern: anxiety, depression, eating disorders.

Twice-expectional children typically have very asynchronous developmental profiles, because the strengths are often very strong, and the challenges are often very challenging. An important perspective to have when supporting 2e children is to see the child for their strengths, and then support them in strengthening their weaknesses. It is not unusual for 2e children to find school a difficult place:

See the child for their strengths and then support them in strengthening their weaknesses. Gifted twice-exceptional students are often difficult to identify. Their difficulty, rather than their gifted knowledge, is often the focus of assessment. The characteristics of giftedness are frequently hidden by low levels of academic achievement.

Your student might know they think and learn well in some subject areas and their knowledge and skills are valued, often in non-academic areas. They may also know they find subjects like maths and English difficult.

Social and emotional challenges can also pose challenges. Sometimes children might not feel secure at school, or they might find it hard to make friends.

Supporting 2e students to thrive

Every child has the right to be happy and successful at school, regardless of their abilities and challenges. Under Australian law the 1992 Disability Discrimination Act states that provisions should be made so your students can experience success regardless of their disability. Being singled out and identified as different is many children's worst fear, so as we set up classrooms and develop social and cultural capital in our spaces there are some modifications to the environment that can be done to help all children regulate. This especially helps our 2e students feel safety and thrive in the classroom.

Some key considerations for helping 2e children thrive include:

- Helping your students see the unique value they bring to the world and encouraging them to have confidence in themselves as a human being.
- Your student may be aware that they sometimes think differently from their classmates, and it is okay to think differently, but reinforce to the whole class that every voice has value. Your unicorn may not be able to comprehend how others don't understand in the same way that your other students might not understand how your unicorn does.
- It can be helpful for them to know that difference can be a strength, and they have a unique contribution to make.
- Success is not just about high grades in every subject.
- Improvement over outcomes is important.

Twice-exceptional students, are often characterised as highly intelligent students who struggle in school due to an invisible learning disability, or sensory integration disorder. These gifted and talented children often fly under the radar, and many teachers fail to recognise their potential. Learning how to identify twice-exceptional students helps teachers find ways for these children to flourish and make the most of their gifts.

Identifying 2e students

So how do we identify these unique students? What observations can help us to uncover the unicorn?

Twice-exceptional children usually display several of the following strengths:

- Creativity
- Sophisticated sense of humour
- Wide range of interests
- Advanced ideas
- Excellent vocabulary
- Special talents that consume their attention.

Twice-exceptional students also tend to face two or more of the following challenges:

- Frustration
- Argumentative personalities
- Poor written expression
- Sensitivity to criticism

- Poor organisational skills
- Poor study habits
- Stubbornness
- Difficulty in social situations.

A child who has some of these traits combined with the above strengths probably has a sophisticated intellect that gets overlooked because of problems with behaviour or expression.

Look at all the masking! Our 2e students should not have to hide! Masking is something very common in the 2e community especially present with neurodivergent students and specifically female students, who want to fit in at any cost. Masking is the act of observing responses and body language, vocal tone, word choices of the peer group and replicating these words, phrases and actions.

As you can imagine masking is exhausting as it is a mental process of matching what your peers are doing rather than just being yourself and your normal. Masking in younger children can present as blow ups at the end of the day, as mental fatigue has set in. Second guessing and roleplaying conversations in your head before and after to ensure that your words will not alienate you from the pack. This masking will take a toll academically as well, 'playing dumb' can ensure that you don't stand out.

- **Lazy.** These children are likely to have been identified as gifted as they generally perform well on tests for academics or giftedness, but they may not do well in gifted programs. They don't do the extra that they are capable of, some don't do the minimum of standard class work required. Some educators will have experienced the frustration of them doing the work, but not submitting it. People may look at them as being lazy or underachievers when they don't perform as well as their hard-working peers.
- **Behaviour difficulty.** These children are less likely to have been identified as gifted because they don't perform well on the gifted identification tests. They could mess around in class, be argumentative or disruptive. I have always argued that standardised testing, test standardised people. Further, because they are sometimes placed in resource rooms or receive other services for their disability, they may become bored, act out, and are more likely to be labelled as a behaviour problem.

- **Disability seen first.** These students are likely to appear as average or slightly below average in the classroom setting. Their abilities and disabilities have an effect of cancelling each other out, making them quite difficult to identify for both their giftedness and their potential learning difficulty or disability. These students become the adults that reflect on teachers words 'this child will never amount to anything'. Also known as the deficit model.

A diagnosis of ADHD or Autism can all too often overwhelm the giftedness diagnosis with a child. If you look at Katy Higgins visual on the next page, the overlap with giftedness is obvious.

The common threads are boredom, intense curiosity and sensitivities probably related to Piechowski's 'gifted overexcitabilities' (1979). Asynchrony's development applies to non 2e gifted students, but they too can be gifted in one, two or many areas. They are often outraged by actions they see as unfair or unjust. They often prefer to work alone and like to learn in their own often quirky ways.

As a so called 'expert' in the field of gifted education I am constantly asking teachers to see beyond what they see as deficit learning and look for the unicorn sticking out in the gifted student.

Figure 2: Highlights the Overlap of Gifted Students and 2e Students. ADHD and Autism Being the Most Commonly Identified 2e Learners.

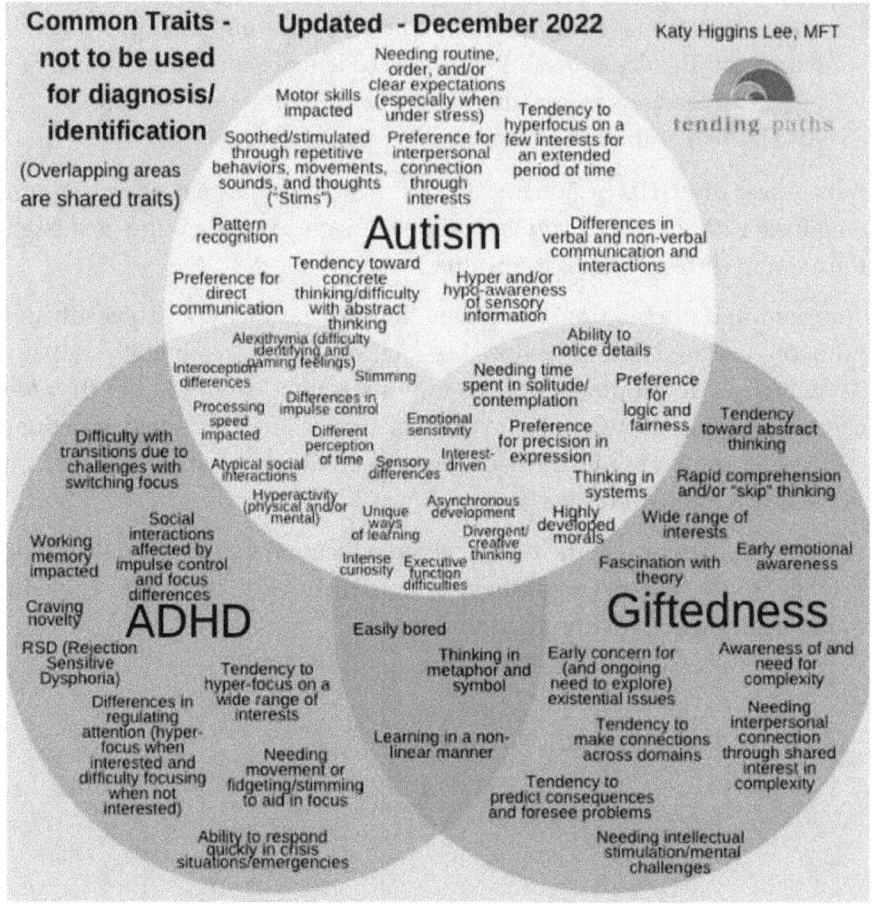

For educators and support teams, the task within this unique zone is both complex and rewarding. It necessitates a tailored and holistic approach that recognises and nurtures the students' exceptional abilities while simultaneously addressing their specific learning challenges. This involves a deep understanding of each student's individual profile, strengths, and weaknesses. As an educator, you're constantly adapting your teaching to meet the needs of your classroom, but it can be difficult to know everything necessary for effectively supporting your students, including those with learning disabilities.

Teachers usually need more guidance in helping gifted students with learning disabilities. There are specific challenges teachers face, such as classroom differentiation accommodations, identifying giftedness and learning disabilities early on, or navigating IEPs (see chapter 3). Maybe you're looking for help with differentiated instruction, inclusive teaching practices, or strategies for fostering social-emotional growth in these students.

So how do you spot a unicorn in the wilds of a noisy classroom?

Here are some strategies teachers can use to help identify 2e students:

- **Conduct informal observations:** Teachers can observe students' behaviour, engagement, and interactions in the classroom. Look for signs of asynchronous development, such as a significant gap between a student's abilities and their performance in certain areas.
- **Review previous records:** Thoroughly review a student's academic and developmental history, including Individualised Education Plans (IEPs), or other documentation of learning challenges. This can provide valuable insights into a student's strengths and weaknesses.
- **Use formal assessments:** If you think there is a difference about a learner, send them to an educational psychologist who can administer both cognitive and academic assessments to identify variations in a student's abilities. Traditional assessments may not accurately reflect a 2e student's true potential.
- **Talk to parents:** Collaborate with parents or guardians to gather information about a student's strengths, challenges, and any previous assessments or diagnoses. Parents often have valuable insights into their child's abilities and behaviours outside school.
- **Look for discrepancies:** Pay attention to significant differences between a student's performance in different subject areas. A 2e student may excel in one area while struggling in another.
- **Use alternative assessment methods:** Consider alternative forms of assessment, such as project-based assessments, portfolio reviews, or performance tasks, which may better capture a 2e student's abilities.
- **Encourage self-reflection:** Foster self-awareness in students by encouraging them to reflect on their own strengths and challenges. This can help students better understand their own learning profiles.

- **Monitor progress:** Continuously monitor students' progress and adjust instructional strategies as needed. Look for changes in performance and behaviour that may indicate areas of strength or struggle. Look for differences in behaviour and achievement after the modifications and adaptions on tasks are put in place.

Remember that identifying 2e students requires a multifaceted approach and a deep understanding of their unique learning profiles. Collaboration among educators, parents, and specialists is crucial in ensuring that these students receive the support and opportunities they need to thrive academically and socially.

Research in the field of twice-exceptionality has shed light on the diverse needs of these students and the strategies that can facilitate their educational journey. It emphasises the importance of early identification, individualised education plans, accommodations, and a supportive learning environment that fosters their potential. Ultimately, by embracing the complexity of twice-exceptional students, educators and researchers alike are working to unlock the full range of their talents and abilities, ensuring they reach their highest potential in both their areas of giftedness and areas of challenge.

Myths and misconceptions

Before embarking on our quest to further identify 2e students, we must first dispel the myths and misconceptions that shroud them. It's common for these students to fly under the radar due to stereotypes and assumptions. We'll examine these misconceptions and arm you with the tools to see beyond them.

2e students are always high achievers	One common misconception is that 2e students are always at the top of their class academically. Their learning disabilities or challenges can mask their giftedness, leading to underachievement in certain areas. A study published in the "Journal for the Education of the Gifted" (Moon & Brighton, 2008) highlights that 2e students often exhibit significant variations in achievement across subjects, contributing to their invisibility in traditional gifted programs.

Giftedness and learning disabilities are mutually exclusive	Another misconception is the belief that giftedness and learning disabilities cannot coexist. In truth, gifted students can have specific learning difficulties or disabilities. According to the National Association for Gifted Children (NAGC), 2e students often exhibit a 'twice-exceptional paradox' where their giftedness and disabilities can mask each other, making it essential to use alternative assessment methods to identify their unique profiles.
2e students are just lazy or unmotivated	Some may assume that 2e students underperform due to laziness or lack of motivation. However, their challenges may result in frustration, anxiety, and a reluctance to engage in tasks they find difficult. Studies by researchers such as Dr Susan Baum and Dr Robin Schader (2000) emphasise the importance of recognising the emotional and social challenges faced by 2e students, which can impact their motivation and achievement.
One-size-fits-all identification methods	Identifying 2e students using traditional assessments alone may overlook their abilities and challenges. Relying solely on standardised tests may not capture their full potential. The "Journal of Psychoeducational Assessment" (Silverman, 2005) highlights the limitations of standardised assessments in identifying 2e students and underscores the importance of using alternative methods like portfolio assessment and teacher observations.

Navigating the identification maze

The first step in identifying 2e students is understanding the diverse range of abilities and challenges they may exhibit. From prodigious talents in mathematics to extraordinary artistic expression, and from struggles with executive functioning to sensitivities that may be mistaken for behavioural issues – we'll explore the spectrum of traits that might indicate twice exceptionality.

- **Asynchronous development:** 2e students often display uneven development, where their intellectual abilities outpace their emotional or social maturity. This asynchrony can lead to unique challenges in the classroom. In a study published in *Gifted Child Quarterly* (Neihart, 1999), asynchronous development was identified as a hallmark trait of 2e students, emphasising the importance of recognising these disparities.
- **Inconsistency in performance:** 2e students may demonstrate significant variations in their academic performance across subjects. They can excel in areas of strength while struggling with tasks that challenge them. The *Journal for the Education of the Gifted* (Rizza & Morrison, 2003) notes that inconsistency in performance is a common trait among 2e students, making their identification more complex.
- **Intense interests:** Many 2e students have intense passions or interests in specific topics. They may immerse themselves in these areas, demonstrating advanced knowledge and skills. Research by Dr Susan Assouline and Dr Nicholas Colangelo (2000) published in *Gifted Child Quarterly* highlights that 2e students often display intense interests and may exhibit expertise in particular domains.
- **Perfectionism:** Some 2e students exhibit perfectionist tendencies, setting exceptionally high standards for themselves. They may become frustrated or anxious when they perceive their performance as falling short of these standards. The *Journal of Learning Disabilities* (Baum et al., 2008) underscores that perfectionism can be a characteristic trait among 2e students, impacting their motivation and self-esteem.
- **Sensory sensitivities:** Many 2e students may have heightened sensory sensitivities, which can include sensitivities to noise, textures, or visual stimuli. These sensitivities can impact their comfort in various environments. Research in *Exceptional Children* (Reis, Neu & McGuire, 1995) highlights that sensory sensitivities are observed in a significant number of 2e students, affecting their classroom experiences.
- **Executive functioning challenges:** Executive functioning skills, such as organisation, time management, and planning, can be areas of difficulty for 2e students. They may struggle to initiate tasks or manage their responsibilities. Studies published in *Gifted Child Today* (Gross, 2004) emphasise that executive functioning challenges are common among 2e students and can impact their academic performance.

- **Heightened emotional sensitivity:** 2e students often exhibit heightened emotional sensitivity, experiencing intense emotions more profoundly than their peers. They may be highly empathetic and compassionate. Research by Dr Linda Silverman (2000) published in *Journal of Learning Disabilities* discusses the emotional intensity often seen in 2e students, emphasising its role in their social and emotional experiences.

If checklists are easier for your teachers, then the following may help.

Identification checklist for 2e students

Here is an easy-to-use checklist:

High intellectual abilities:
- ☐ Demonstrates advanced problem-solving skills.
- ☐ Shows curiosity and a deep understanding of complex concepts.
- ☐ Excels in specific subjects or areas (e.g., mathematics, art, science).

Learning challenges:
- ☐ Struggles with reading, writing, or arithmetic despite high intelligence.
- ☐ Exhibits signs of ADHD, dyslexia, autism spectrum disorder, or other learning disabilities.
- ☐ Inconsistent academic performance, excelling in some areas while struggling in others.

Asynchronous development:
- ☐ Displays uneven development across differing domains (e.g., advanced verbal skills but delayed motor skills).
- ☐ They experience frustration or boredom in areas where they excel but have difficulty in areas of challenge.

Social and emotional traits:
- ☐ Shows signs of emotional intensity or sensitivity.
- ☐ Experiences difficulties with social interactions and forming peer relationships.
- ☐ Demonstrates perfectionism and fear of failure.

Behavioural characteristics:
- ☐ Exhibits intense focus and passion for specific interests.

- ☐ Shows signs of underachievement or disengagement in school.
- ☐ Experiences frequent frustration or emotional outbursts related to academic tasks.

How to support and advocate for your gifted student

Here are some ideas:

Educational strategies:
- Ensure your student has an Individualised Education Plan (IEP) that addresses both their strengths and challenges.
- Advocate for differentiated instruction and flexible teaching methods in the classroom for twice-exceptional students.

Strength-based approach:
- Encourage your child to pursue their passions and interests.
- Provide opportunities for enrichment activities that align with their strengths.
- Focus on building self-confidence through positive reinforcement and celebrating achievements.

Therapeutic and counselling support:
- Seek out psychologists and other professionals who specialise in working with gifted and twice-exceptional children.
- Consider occupational therapy, speech and language therapy, or other specialised services to address specific challenges.
- Provide social and emotional support through counselling or peer support groups.

Parental involvement:
- Ensure that parents are informed about twice-exceptional education and best practices.
- Maintain open communication with teachers, counsellors, and therapists.
- Encourage parents and carers to create a supportive home environment that fosters both academic and emotional growth.

Resources:
- Ask for professional learning on twice-exceptional children.

- Attend workshops, conferences, and support groups related to twice-exceptionality.
- Connect with professional organisations and utilise resources from organisations

Identifying 2e students often requires a multidimensional approach that goes beyond qualitative testing. We'll delve into the complexities of assessment, including the need for comprehensive evaluations that capture both giftedness and challenges. By combining cognitive, academic, and socioemotional assessments, we can create a more accurate portrait of these unique learners. Bringing in specialists such as educational psychologists can be beneficial, each method of assessment and profile building has its own set of pros and cons, the list below is not exhaustive, just the most common form of identification.

- **Psychoeducational assessment:** Psychoeducational assessments involve standardised tests that measure cognitive abilities, academic achievement, and social-emotional functioning. These assessments may include IQ tests, academic achievement tests, and behaviour rating scales.

  Pros: Provides a baseline of cognitive functioning, identifies specific learning disabilities or giftedness, and highlights areas of academic strength and weakness.

  Cons: May not capture the full range of a 2e student's abilities, as some gifted areas may not be assessed. It may also miss nuances of social-emotional struggles.

- **Observational assessment:** Observational assessments involve close observation of a student's behaviour and interactions in various contexts, including the classroom and social settings.

  Pros: Offers valuable insights into a 2e student's social interactions, emotional regulation, and executive functioning skill. Provides context for understanding behaviours.

  Cons: Subjective and may be influenced by the observer's bias. Limited to what can be observed during the assessment period.

- **Portfolio assessment:** Portfolio assessments involve collecting and reviewing a 2e student's work samples over time, including assignments, projects, and creative endeavours.

Pros: Showcases a 2e student's strengths and areas of interest, capturing their creative and intellectual potential. Provides a holistic view of their abilities.

Cons: Time-consuming to compile and assess portfolios.

- **Dynamic assessment:** Dynamic assessments involve interacting with a 2e student through tasks or activities that adapt based on their responses. The goal is to assess their potential for learning and problem-solving.

    Pros: Measures a student's ability to learn and adapt, rather than focusing solely on current skills. Can identify areas of strength masked by learning difficulties.

    Cons: Requires specialised training for administrators. May be less standardised, making it challenging to compare results.

- **Checklists and rating scales:** Checklists and rating scales involve surveys or questionnaires completed by teachers, parents, and the student themselves to assess various aspects of behaviour, emotions, and executive functioning.

    Identifying twice-exceptional children is rarely a straightforward process. All children have their own gifts, but they also have their own struggles. The high number of combinations makes it difficult to pinpoint a single way to identify gifted children with disabilities.

    Twice-exceptional children are often identified when they show promise in one or two areas. ADHD may make it difficult for a child to answer math and reading questions, but that child may excel when it comes to solving real-world problems like figuring out puzzles or finding creative solutions.

    Educators may also identify twice-exceptional students by recognising a decline in performance. A child may do very well in class before succumbing to difficulties created by a learning disability. If the child's performance begins to slip, teachers should take a closer look to determine whether an outside influence is contributing to lower grades. Declining performance can also come from poor eyesight, hearing and other physical problems.

    Pros: Provide a broader perspective by collecting input from multiple sources. Can identify social and emotional challenges.

    Cons: Subjective and reliant on the accuracy of responses. Limited by the respondent's knowledge and understanding.

- **Functional Behaviour Assessment (FBA):** Usually you need your learning diversity head to action this assessment or another professional like a psychologis. FBAs focus on identifying the function or purpose of a 2e student's challenging behaviours. This assessment helps determine why certain behaviours occur.

    Pros: Provides a deeper understanding of a student's behaviours and can guide interventions to address specific issues.

    Cons: Requires specialised training to conduct. May not assess academic or cognitive abilities directly.

Moving away from labels and towards recognising signs in 2e students offers numerous advantages. While labels can be helpful for schools in navigating adjustments and providing targeted support, they can also be limiting and stigmatising. Embracing signs rather than labels allows for a more holistic understanding of a student's strengths and challenges. It encourages educators to focus on individualised strategies rather than pigeonholing students into predefined categories. Moreover, this approach empowers 2e individuals to better understand themselves without being constrained by societal stereotypes associated with labels. It promotes a growth mindset, where learners are encouraged to explore new interests and abilities without the fear of being confined by rigid expectations. Ultimately, this shift fosters a more inclusive and supportive environment that celebrates the uniqueness and potential of each 2e student (Silverman, 2013).

A useful list to support 2e students

Students with ADHD can concentrate better when they're allowed to fidget. Not only is this a useful list for teachers of 2e ADHD students but gifted students in general all tend to 'fidget' or become restless and bored. The intersection with Piechowski's 'gifted overexcitabilities' is really strong here and you may wish to pursue it. I often think they are so closely aligned that misdiagnosis of ADHD is a strong possibility.

Practical and physical supports are subjective and specific to each student. Some practical supports could include:

1. **Squeeze balls:** Squishy balls, stress balls, koosh balls, hand exercisers... there are dozens of objects that can be squeezed quietly. Teacher tip: Make sure that children use them under their

desks for minimal distractions to others. Fun activity idea: Fill balloons up with different items (seeds, Play-Doh, flour, etc.) to squish.

2. **Fidgets:** Fidgets are small objects that help keep students' hands occupied. You can buy these on Amazon or use objects like beaded bracelets or Rubik's cubes. Teacher tip: Avoid flashy objects like fidget spinners, which can be a distraction to other students.

3. **Silly putty:** Silly putty, Play-Doh, or sticky tack can also keep students' hands occupied.

4. **Velcro:** Tape a strip of the rough side of Velcro under the student's desk. It gives them something to touch. Many other objects can work, such as emery boards or straws.

5. **Gum or chewable necklaces:** Chewing gum can help keep some ADHD students focused. In no-gum classrooms, necklaces with chewable pieces can also work. You can also wrap airline tubing or rubber bands at the ends of pencils for students to chew.

6. **Doodling:** Doodling can help many students focus. Some gifted students also benefit if they can draw during story time or a lesson.

7. **Background white noise and music:** A fan in the back of the room can help some students focus. Letting them listen to music on headphones (as long as it doesn't interfere with what's happening in class) can also help. One teacher had success with an aquarium in the back of the room – students liked hearing the calming swish of the water.

8. **Chair leg bands:** Tie a large rubber band (or yoga band) across both front legs of the chair for students to push or pull against with their legs.

9. **Bouncy balls:** Also known as yoga balls, stability balls, or exercise balls. These are potentially great for all students, not just ones with ADHD.

10. **Swivel chairs:** Children can twist a little bit from side to side. A rocking chair also works.

11. **Wobble chairs:** Similar to swivel chairs or disk seats, these chairs let students rock within their seats. Teacher tip: Don't let students wobble too much – they may fall off!

12. **Disk seats:** These sit on a chair and allow students to rock in their seats, which is not as dangerous as rocking the entire chair. Cushions can also work.

13. **Standing desks:** Great for all students, not just ones who need to fidget.

14. **Desks with swinging footrests:** A built-in footrest can help reduce the noise that comes with foot tapping.

15. **Stationary bikes:** Putting a stationary bicycle at the back of the classroom is a great way to help students be active.
16. **Classroom space for moving around:** Clear an area at the side or back of the room to let students stand, stretch, dance, pace, or twirl.
17. **Flexible work locations:** Students don't have to do their learning at their desk – they can work at the windowsill or move from one desk to another. Having different learning stations can benefit all types of students.
18. **Smell:** Some classrooms can benefit from calming, clean neutral smells. As a teacher avoid lighting candles. Wax melts using electronic devices, diffusers and reeds are safer, if you know you have a unicorn sensitive to smell, check fragrances that are tolerated, vanilla, lemon, citrus, peppermint and lavender are often considered neutral.

It should be noted that these interventions can help, but they are not a cure. They allow space for 2e students to utilise more cognitive-based therapies and strategies developed in conjunction with educational and psychological professionals. It is also challenging to use many of these strategies in secondary classrooms, so speak to your secondary students privately about strategies which are known to work for them.

Speaking of environments

Creating an environment that encourages 2e students to reveal their true colours is a key part of identification. Teachers need to foster a safe and inclusive classroom where students feel comfortable expressing their strengths and challenges. By establishing trust and rapport, you'll increase the likelihood of uncovering the 2e gems in your midst.

Try to:

- Foster a growth mindset.
- Encourage risk-taking and learning from mistakes.
- Promote resilience, emphasising that setbacks are part of the learning process.

Armed with a deeper understanding of the complexity of 2e learners and the tools to identify them, you're ready to embark on your unicorn hunt. As you hone your observation skills and broaden your perspective, you'll unveil the hidden potential and brilliance of these exceptional students – the ones who, once unmasked, can transform your classroom into a realm of endless possibilities. So all of this information is useful but what can the teacher do in the classroom to assist optimal learning for 2e students?

Practical ideas for catering for 2e students over the years

Step	Primary School	Secondary School
Create a welcoming environment	Arrange colourful, age-appropriate decor.	Use engaging bulletin boards and age-appropriate decorations.
Establish clear expectations	Develop simple, visual classroom rules.	Collaboratively create classroom norms with students.
Build positive relationships	Use icebreakers and games to foster connections.	Incorporate team-building activities to build trust among students.
Differentiate instruction	Tailor lessons to various learning styles and abilities.	Provide flexible learning options and challenges for diverse learners.
Encourage open communication	Promote active listening and empathy.	Foster respectful debates and discussions.
Address behavioural issues	Implement a behaviour management system, like a token economy.	Use restorative justice practices to address behaviour. Use social stories and stories that highlight others perspectives.
Offer supportive Resources	Provide a cozy reading corner and age-appropriate materials.	Create a resource-rich classroom with access to books, technology, and reference materials.
Celebrate achievements	Hold weekly awards or recognition ceremonies.	Recognise student achievements through student-led assemblies or awards.
Embrace inclusive practices	Promote inclusivity through collaborative projects and activities.	Encourage inclusion through group work and diverse perspectives.

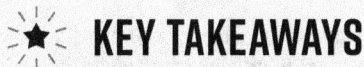# KEY TAKEAWAYS

- **The unique complexity of twice exceptionality (2e):** Twice-exceptional students possess both exceptional strengths, such as advanced intellectual or creative abilities, and significant challenges, such as learning disabilities or neurodiversity. This duality often masks their true potential, making them difficult to identify and support effectively in traditional educational settings.

- **Barriers to identification:** Many schools and educators focus on deficits rather than strengths when assessing students, often overlooking 2e individuals. Misdiagnoses, limited testing tools, and societal biases further complicate the recognition of these "unicorns", leaving their unique needs unmet.

- **Strength-based approach in classrooms:** Supporting 2e learners requires shifting from deficit-based interventions to a strengths-focused approach. Emphasising their interests, talents, and abilities while addressing their challenges fosters emotional wellbeing, confidence, and academic growth.

- **Challenges of masking:** 2e students, particularly neurodiverse ones, often "mask" their struggles to blend in socially, leading to exhaustion and underachievement. Teachers must create safe, inclusive environments where these students feel comfortable expressing their authentic selves.

- **Practical strategies for educators:** Identifying and supporting 2e students involves a multifaceted approach, including observing classroom behaviours, fostering open communication, offering differentiated instruction, and creating inclusive environments. Tools like flexible workspaces, fidget options and sensory accommodations can further enhance learning for these unique students.

Chapter references

Assouline, S. G., & Colangelo, N. (2000). Counseling gifted students. In K. A. Heller, F. J. Mönks, R. J. Sternberg, & R. F. Subotnik (Eds.), *International handbook of giftedness and talent* (2nd ed., pp. 595–607). Elsevier.

Australian Bureau of Statistics. (2020). *Data on gifted students in Australia*. Retrieved from https://www.abs.gov.au

Baum, S., & Schader, R. (2000). Understanding and supporting twice-exceptional learners. *Gifted Child Quarterly, 44*(3), 152–162. https://doi.org/10.1177/001698620604400301

Baum, S., Schader, R., & Hébert, T. P. (2008). Strength-based approaches to twice-exceptionality: Supporting gifted students with disabilities. *Journal of Learning Disabilities, 41*(5), 396–408. https://doi.org/10.1177/0022219408317796

Gross, M. U. M. (2004). Exceptionally gifted children: Long-term outcomes of acceleration and non-acceleration. *Gifted Child Today, 42*(4), 19–35. https://doi.org/10.1177/1076217518804856

Moon, S. M., & Brighton, C. M. (2008). Understanding the paradox of twice exceptionality. *Journal for the Education of the Gifted, 31*(4), 399–430. https://doi.org/10.1177/016235320803100403

National Association for Gifted Children. (n.d.). *Twice-exceptional learners*. Retrieved from https://www.nagc.org

Neihart, M. (1999). The impact of asynchronous development on gifted learners. *Gifted Child Quarterly, 43*(3), 161–171. https://doi.org/10.1177/001698629904300306

Nikakis, S. (2023). Understanding twice-exceptional learners: A comprehensive guide for educators. *Gifted Education International, 39*(2), 145–158.

Reis, S. M., Neu, T. W., & McGuire, J. M. (1995). Talent in two worlds: Supporting twice-exceptional learners. *Exceptional Children, 61*(6), 430–441. https://doi.org/10.1177/001440299506100601

Rizza, M. G., & Morrison, W. F. (2003). Uncovering stereotypes and identifying characteristics of gifted students and students with emotional/behavioral disabilities. *Roeper Review, 25*(2), 73–77.

Silverman, L. K. (2000). Identifying visual-spatial and auditory-sequential learners: A validation study. In N. Colangelo & S. G. Assouline (Eds.), Talent development V: Proceedings from the 2000 Henry B. and Jocelyn Wallace National Research Symposium on Talent Development (pp. 247–265). Gifted Psychology Press.

Silverman, L. K. (2005). *Upside-down brilliance: The visual-spatial learner*. The Institute for the Study of Advanced Development.

Silverman, L. K. (2013). Embracing the strengths of gifted learners: A call to action for educators. *Journal of Learning Disabilities, 46*(2), 91–102. https://doi.org/10.1177/0022219412456703

CHAPTER 3

IEPs, PLPs and ILPs: More Than Alphabet Soup

Dr Susan Nikakis

Understanding IEPs for twice-exceptional students

With your unicorn in sight, (see chapter 2), it's time to embark on the journey of providing tailored support to twice-exceptional (2e) students. This chapter is all about crafting individualised education plans that go beyond mere acronyms or alphabet mania – IEPs (Individualised Education Plans) and ILPs (Individualised Learning Plans). These plans are the tools that can bridge the gap between potential and achievement for 2e learners. The most important asset to twice-exceptional gifted students are teachers!

Twice-exceptional learners have been defined as possessing the capacity for high achievement, in addition to having a disability (Joint Commission on Twice-Exceptional Students, 2009). The term is commonly used to describe students who are both gifted in one or more domains (mathematics, science, technology, social art, visual, spatial, performing arts) and have a disability which may be cognitive, physical, and/or emotional (Assouline et al., 2010; Nicpon, et al., 2011; Missett, 2017).

Twice-exceptional students often face challenges stemming from misconception, misidentification, or misplacement in educational systems (Foley-Nicpon & Candler, 2018). Because the disability may mask the gift/talent domain or the gift/talent domain may mask the disability, it can be challenging to recognise these students and appropriately respond to their learning needs (Baldwin et al., 2015).

It has become apparent that this misconception can contribute to the under identification for educational curriculum planning of gifted children with co-existing disabilities – the twice-exceptional.

The *Melbourne Declaration (2008)* espouses the dual goals of equity and excellence. Excellence requires all students to have access to a curriculum that encourages high expectations of all learners.

Each state and territory have processes in place to identify gifted and talented learners and to meet the goals of the Melbourne Declaration. Schools can also use the three dimensions of the Australian Curriculum to develop effective gifted and talented programs.

Teachers also have a legal duty to meet the needs of twice-exceptional students in their care. The Melbourne Declaration of Educational Goals for Young Australians (MCEETYA, 2008) states that teachers have a duty of care to provide equitable access to high quality schooling with stimulating learning experiences which take into account a student's diverse learning needs.

Also, a 2e child who has some of these traits combined with the above strengths probably has a sophisticated intellect that gets overlooked because of problems with behaviour or expression. Children who have these skills, but perform poorly at school, are often twice exceptional. An IEP which is well designed and appropriate can assist both teacher and student. Note that not all gifted students require an IEP but all twice exceptional students should have one to ensure that teachers are aware of the giftedness aspect of the IEP.

Up to 30 per cent of gifted students display a learning disability, with 10 percent reading at two or more years below their grade level. They are referred to as being 'gifted learning disabled' or as having the dual exceptionalities of giftedness and learning disabilities. For these students, their learning disability is more likely to be recognised and targeted in teaching than their gifted ability. An IEP can keep the giftedness at the forefront.

The profile of a gifted student does not typically include disabilities. The ability of a child to be both learning disabled and gifted is a paradigm which confuses many educators, parents and students. To many, these are mutually exclusive categories and to possess both is either a mistake or unbelievable. An understanding of the complexities of twice-exceptional students is paramount to be able to cater to their diverse learning needs, so that both disability and gifts are given the attention they deserve.

Individualised Education Plans (IEP)

IEPs can be a useful adjunct to enhancing the learning needs of 2e students. IEPs assist students who require a range of supports with their education.

An IEP is a written statement that describes the adjustments, goals and strategies to meet a student's individual educational needs so they can reach their full potential. An IEP is essential as it helps educators plan and monitor a student's unique learning needs.

IEPs are also known as individual learning plans, individual learning improvement plans and Koorie education learning plans.

Teachers already undertake many activities that personalise learning experiences for students. Research has shown that when schools use a planning approach that supports personalised learning, the academic achievement of all students improves.

Planning Goals for an IEP – in other words ideas for teachers to write on the IEP

Given training in and visual reminders of self-regulatory scripts student will manage unexpected events and violations of routine without disrupting classroom activities.

The student will use a structured recipe or routine for generating new ideas or brainstorming to respond successfully to open-ended assignments.

When faced with changes and/or transitions in activities or environments, the student can initiate the new activity after (decreasing the number of supports).

Given concrete training, visual supports and fading adult cuing, the student can appropriately label flexible and stuck behaviours in himself.

Given training and practice with the concept of compromise, and in the presence of visual supports, the student can accept and generate compromise solutions to conflicts when working cooperatively with others.

Pre IEP-meeting preparation

Review student's current IEP
- Read through the current IEP document.
- Make notes on areas of progress and areas needing improvement.

Initiate triennial evaluation process
- Send a letter or email to parents to inform them about the upcoming IEP meeting.
- Obtain parental consent.

Gather existing data and assessments
- Collect academic performance data.
- Obtain progress reports from all relevant teachers and service providers.
- Review recent assessment results (both formal and informal).

Conduct comprehensive evaluations
- Arrange for the necessary evaluations (cognitive, academic, speech, language, occupational therapy, physical therapy, etc.).
- Ensure all evaluations are completed in a timely manner.
- Collect input from all team members regarding the student's current performance and needs.

Consult with specialists
- Meet with special education teachers, therapists, and any other involved specialists to discuss the student's progress and needs.

Parent communication
- Send a meeting invitation to parents at least seven days in advance.
- Provide parents with a draft agenda and any data or reports to be discussed.
- Ask parents if they have any specific concerns or topics they want to address. This is VERY important as it makes the parents feel included.

Schedule meeting
- Ensure the availability of all necessary team members (general education teacher, special education teacher, related service providers, etc.).
- Confirm the meeting date, time, and location with all participants.

During the IEP meeting

Introductions and agenda review
- Introduce all team members.
- Review the **agenda** and purpose.

Review IEP information
- Present the results of the gathered information.
- Discuss how the evaluation results impact the student's learning.

Review student's progress
- Discuss the student's progress
- Share data and observations from various team members.

Parental input
- Provide parents with an opportunity to share their observations and concerns.
- Address any specific questions or topics raised by parents.

Develop new goals
- Based on the student's progress and current needs, develop new IEP goals.
- Ensure goals are specific, measurable, achievable, relevant, and time-bound (SMART).

Determine services and accommodations
- Discuss necessary educational services and related services.
- Review and update accommodations and modifications as needed.
- For students approaching a transition (e.g., moving to a different grade level or preparing for post-secondary life), develop a transition plan.
- Ensure the plan includes steps for achieving goals.
- It is important to include the student in some aspects of the discussions.

IEP meeting follow-up

Finalise IEP document
- Complete and finalise the IEP document based on meeting discussions.
- Ensure all team members, including parents, sign the IEP.

Distribute final IEP
- Provide a copy of the final IEP to parents and all relevant team members.
- Ensure all service providers have access to the IEP to implement it correctly.

Implement IEP
- Communicate any changes or updates to the student's plan to all teachers and service providers.
- Begin implementing the new goals, services, and accommodations according to the date on the IEP.

Monitor progress
- Regularly check on the student's progress towards IEP goals.
- Schedule periodic check-ins with parents and team members to discuss ongoing progress and any necessary adjustments.

Documentation and record-keeping
- Document all communications with parents and team members.
- Keep detailed records of the IEP meeting, including meeting minutes and decisions made.

Essential components of an effective 2e learning plan

Before diving into the intricacies of these plans, let's demystify the alphabet soup. We'll clarify the differences between IEPs and ILPs, explore their purposes, and emphasise how they can be harnessed to address both giftedness and challenges. By understanding the purpose behind the letters, you'll be better equipped to wield their power.

Crafting effective IEPs and ILPs requires a deep understanding of the individual profiles of 2e students. An education IEP has more of a teacher focus while an lLP is supposed to have the learning of the student as paramount. Education systems in Australia and in other parts of the world use a variety of the acronyms as interchangeable. Needless to say, the student should be part of the preparation of the document but sadly this is not always the case.

IEP (Individual Education Plan), PLP (Personalised Learning Program) or ILP (Individual Learning Program)

An IEP is a written plan which describes the adjustments, goals and strategies to meet a student's individual educational needs so they can reach their full potential.

An IEP can provide teachers with accessible information about twice-exceptional diagnoses and suggested accommodations, modifications, and collaboration with other educational professionals. An IEP is essential as it helps you plan and monitor a student's unique learning needs. Some education systems have compulsory IEP formats, but they too can be modified.

What makes a good IEP/ILP?

A good Individual Learning Plan (ILP) document is a critical tool in providing personalised education and support for students with diverse needs. Here are key components and characteristics that make an effective ILP document:

- **Student-centred:** The ILP should be tailored to the specific needs, strengths, interests, and goals of the individual student. It should reflect their unique learning style and preferences.
- **Clear and specific goals:** The ILP should include clear, measurable, and achievable academic and/or developmental goals for the student. These goals should be broken down into smaller, actionable steps.
- **Assessment data:** Include relevant assessment data, such as diagnostic tests, evaluations, and observations. This data helps in identifying areas of need and tracking progress over time.
- **Support services:** Outline the support services and accommodations the student requires, such as special education services, counselling, assistive technology, or speech therapy.
- **Timelines:** Establish timelines for achieving the set goals. This helps in tracking progress and ensuring that interventions are implemented in a timely manner.
- **Progress monitoring:** Describe how and when progress will be monitored and measured. This could include regular check-ins, assessments, or benchmarks.
- **Collaborative approach:** Involve teachers, parents/guardians, specialists, and the student (when age-appropriate) in the

development and ongoing review of the ILP. Collaboration ensures that everyone is aligned and working towards the same goals.
- **Flexibility:** An effective ILP should be flexible and adaptable. It should evolve as the student's needs change or as new information becomes available.
- **Communication plan:** Outline how communication will be maintained among all stakeholders. This could include regular meetings, progress reports, or a dedicated point of contact.
- **Legal compliance:** Ensure that the ILP complies with relevant laws and regulations, such as the National Consistent Collection of Data (NCCD) in Australia.

Here is an example of a Personal Learning Plan (PLP) designed by gifted educator Enza Bunetta (MACS).

Record of Program Plan and Consultation for Highly Able Students					
Program Plan						
Name of Student		Date of Birth		Year Level	
E Number		School Name		Date Range of Plan	
Teachers					
Relevant Information e.g. Cognitive Assessment Data					
Most Recent School Data					
Any Other Relevant Information					
Interests/ Motivators					

Program Plan			
Curriculum Content Area and Student Entry Level	Mode of Adjustment for Program Plan (refer Appendix A for examples)	Resources Strategies/ Adjustments Frequency and Duration	Mode of Assessment/ Data Collection Teacher Evaluation
READING Curriculum Level/ Entry point:			
WRITING Curriculum Level/ Entry point:			
SPELLING Entry point:			
MATHS NUMBER & ALGEBRA Curriculum Level: MATHS – M'MENT AND GEOMETRY Curriculum Level: MATHS – STATISTICS & PROBABILITY Curriculum Level:			
INQUIRY Curriculum Level:			
STEMMS Curriculum Level:			

Use of Technology Tools to Support Output	
Mode of Technology Typing/ voice to text/ recording	**Purpose of Use** (Include curriculum area, type of task and how often)

Consultation

Program Support Group Meeting

Date of Consultation:

In attendance:

Points of Discussion from Consultation:

Key Actions and person/s or team responsible:

Attendees at meeting and plan reviewed and accepted by:

Parent/s, Carer or Guardian	Name:
	Signature:
	Relationship to Student:
Class or Curriculum Area Teacher	Name:
	Signature:
Learning Diversity Leader	Name:
	Signature:
Other	Name:
	Signature:

Models for Program Planning

Gifted strategies		
Strategy	What is it?	Examples
Pre-testing	A way to find out what the student already knows before the teacher starts teaching.	Providing a version of the pre-test. Questioning students verbally.
Curriculum Compacting	A strategy that streamlines and eliminates previously mastered grade-level curriculum for students that are capable of completing content at a faster pace.	Identify the content the students might have mastered by assessing or collecting data. Do not teach what is already mastered.
Acceleration	A strategy that allows the content to be covered at a faster pace than typical.	Whole grade skipping. Subject acceleration.
Grouping	A strategy that groups gifted students with their academic peers, making it easier for teachers to provide enrichment and acceleration.	Ability grouping.
Enrichment	Activities that go beyond the regular classroom.	Diving deeper into the curriculum standard. Designing a science experiment. Proposing an alternate assignment – with real outcomes.
Academic Competitions	A strategy that can be incorporated as a club, enrichment cluster, or curriculum for a gifted class.	STEM Mad. Tournament of the Minds.

With thanks to MACS' Enza Bunetta.

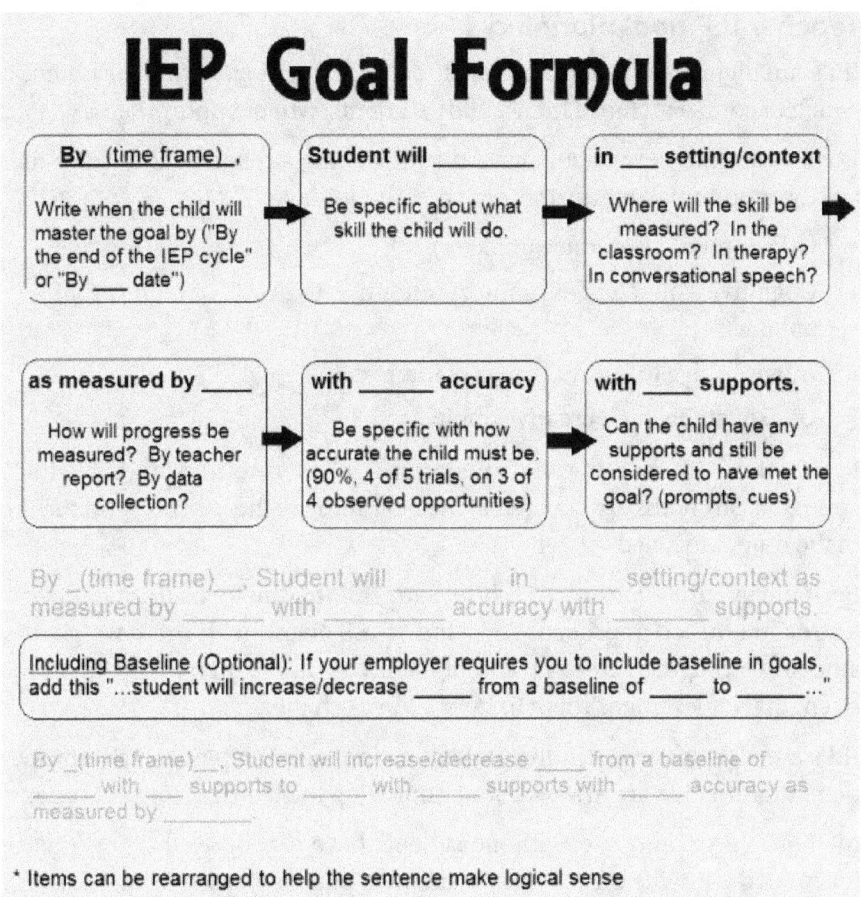

I started my teaching career using a basic business tool called an 'IEP Goal Formula'. While it was not designed for students and learning goals it was a good start for me as a young teacher, so I modified the document. If you are creating your own version, may I suggest a working party including students to interrogate the model thoroughly.

Teacher IEP goal planning

IEPs are highly recommended for students not achieving to their potential which of course includes high-ability students, where appropriate.

Remember that 2e students have distinguishing strengths. They have high ability or potential in one or more areas, including:

- One or more academic subject(s).
- Cognitive skills such as memory, attention to detail, or high verbal abilities.
- Intense drive to learn in areas of interest.
- Unexpectedly high creative ability.

In a typical IEP meeting, not much time is given to looking at a child's strengths. Strengths are covered at the beginning of the meeting and the rest of the time is focused on deficits.

Fortunately, more and more schools are shifting the focus from deficits to a strengths-based approach. This kind of IEP gives much more weight to a student's strengths, interests, and preferences. The team not only identifies strengths but leverages them to help address challenges.

IEPs are also known as individual education learning plans, ILPs however no matter the title are always about improving the learning for the student.

Melbourne Archdiocese Catholic schools have a good example primarily for funded students on NCCD. On the next page is the Victorian DET high ability section of its IEP.

FUNCTIONAL AREA *Roll your mouse over the "thought bubble" for further information.	Current strengths	Identified focus	Date Reviewed	Adjustments required to address the identified need (include frequency –infrequent/occasional action or frequent low level action within class, at specific times, on most days at most times, at all times)
Communication				
Social				
Processing				
Sensory				
Behaviour/Safety				
Personal Care				
Physical				
Health				
Curriculum				

Do all 2e students need an ILP?

No, only where personalised learning and support is required. The Student Support Group (SSG) assisting the student may need to prioritise goals, to ensure the student achieves positive educational outcomes.

A basic ILP may look like this if teachers are at the beginning of the process.

Establish long- and short-term goals

Action What will the student do?	Under what conditions? Where, with whom, with what?	Success criteria What does success look like?	By when? Date
Natasha will use SOLO taxonomy as a tool. She will explain it to the rest of the group.	In a room or section of the classroom away from other groups. This is to increase focus on the task.	All sections of the SOLO taxonomy will be complete. The teacher will be interested in the relational aspects.	The progress will be reviewed by week 5.

The Victorian government Department of education has a wonderful visual for inclusive education. This can assist teacher to complete the IEP or PLP if they require extra guidance.

Curiously some educators do not utilise the IEP (which is a reason I start them on an easy version), but it is an excellent vehicle to assist teachers in providing the best education possible for this student.

Implementation and monitoring

Crafting plans is just the beginning. From adjusting lesson plans to providing stimulus let's look at how to bring the plans to life. We'll also cover the importance of ongoing monitoring and adjusting plans as needed.

Caution is required when collating and collecting data! How often are you as a teacher reading, following, implementing IEP strategies, or are you, or your classroom teachers just ticking the boxes?

Remember to triangulate your data. Don't just use one test, or one essay, or one short answer responses. Ensure that your 2e student is having their needs met.

Objectives should include giving greater priority to the skills and attributes required for life and work in the 21st century, including skills in communicating, creating, using technologies, working in teams and problem solving. They should include developing students' deep understandings of essential disciplinary concepts and principles and their ability to apply these understandings to complex, engaging real-world problems.

Diagnosing learning difficulties upon entry to school; and intervening intensively during the early years of school to address individual learning needs to give as many students as possible the chance of successful ongoing learning. IEPs can assist in this process.

IEPs and ILPs are not just documents; they are powerful instruments that can transform the educational experience of 2e students. By creating plans that celebrate their strengths and address their challenges, you're releasing the magic that lies within each of these exceptional learners. As you embark on this journey of personalised support, remember that the true enchantment lies in watching these students thrive, achieve, and realise their full potential.

Why is an IEP important?

An individual education plan is important because it:

- Empowers students, teachers and parents.
- Supports the school and classroom teacher to develop a meaningful learning program for individual students and to track progress against SMART goals.
- Provides an opportunity to share information between school, student, family and other support professionals.
- Helps schools to determine resources required to achieve the student's learning goals.
- Promotes student confidence and engagement through involvement in the process.

Advocating with colleagues for differentiation in the classroom, with schools to provide best practice and with the community to ensure appropriate services are available is a great first step. However, this needs to be done with state and federal legislators to ensure funding is provided and with the general public puting a spotlight on the needs and capabilities of these amazing students. It is essential if we are to truly meet the needs of these exceptional students (Roberts & Siegle, 2012).

The most important asset to twice-exceptional students are teachers: teacher attitudes can significantly influence the outcomes for twice-exceptional students (Chivers, 2012). Teachers who advocate on behalf of these students are the key to unlocking their unlimited potential and ensuring that the iceberg underneath the water can be developed and appreciated.

The contradiction of possessing both high abilities and disabilities is misunderstood and subsequently mistreated, and the result is an ongoing frustration for students and supporters of twice-exceptionality.

Twice-exceptional students are particularly at risk of low self-esteem, poor self-concept and low motivation due to their asynchronous abilities, and any plan to address their needs, must include consideration of their social-emotional functioning (Assouline et al., 2010; Reis et al., 2014). Our ILPs, IEPs or PLPs can assist their unique learning needs.

# KEY TAKEAWAYS

- **Importance of Individualised Education Plans (IEPs):** IEPs and ILPs are critical tools for twice-exceptional (2e) students, offering personalised adjustments, goals, and strategies that address their unique strengths and challenges. Effective IEPs keep both giftedness and disabilities in focus, ensuring that neither is overlooked.

- **Challenges in identifying 2e students:** Many 2e learners remain undetected due to misconceptions, masking of abilities or disabilities, and biases in testing methods. This under identification often leads to unmet learning needs and misaligned educational strategies.

- **Legal and ethical responsibility of educators:** According to frameworks like the Melbourne Declaration (2008), educators have a legal duty to provide equitable, high-quality education tailored to the diverse needs of students, including those who are 2e. This includes recognising their potential and providing stimulating learning experiences.

- **Strength-based approach:** Successful educational plans for 2e students focus on leveraging their unique strengths and gifts while addressing areas of difficulty. By highlighting talents and creating nurturing environments, educators can build self-esteem and encourage academic and personal growth.

- **Collaboration and regular review:** Creating and implementing IEPs is a collaborative process involving teachers, parents, specialists, and the students themselves. Regular reviews ensure plans remain effective, adapting to the evolving needs and progress of the student.

Chapter references

Assouline, S. G., Foley-Nicpon, M., & Whiteman, C. (2010). Cognitive and psychosocial characteristics of gifted students with written language disability. *Gifted Child Quarterly, 54*(2), 102-115. https://doi.org/10.1177/0016986210396436

Australian Bureau of Statistics. (2020). Data on gifted students in Australia. Retrieved from https://www.abs.gov.au

Baldwin, L., Omdal, S. N., & Pereles, D. (2015). Beyond stereotypes: Understanding, recognizing, and working with twice-exceptional learners. *Teaching Exceptional Children, 47*(4), 216-225. https://doi.org/10.1177/0040059915569362

Chivers, S. (2012). Twice-exceptionality in the classroom. *Journal of Student Engagement: Education Matters, 2*(1), 26-29.

Foley-Nicpon, M., & Candler, N. (2018). Twice-exceptionality: Understanding and supporting gifted students with disabilities. *Gifted Child Today, 41*(2), 84-91. https://doi.org/10.1177/1076217517750762

Joint Commission on Twice-Exceptional Students. (2009). Guidelines for understanding and educating twice-exceptional students. *National Association for Gifted Children.*

Melbourne Declaration on Educational Goals for Young Australians. (2008). Ministerial Council on Education, Employment, Training, and Youth Affairs (MCEETYA). Retrieved from http://www.curriculum.edu.au

Missett, T. C. (2017). Twice-exceptional students: Addressing the paradox of strengths and challenges. *Gifted Child Quarterly, 61*(3), 236-249. https://doi.org/10.1177/0016986217701838

Nicpon, M. F., Allmon, A., Sieck, B., & Stinson, R. D. (2011). Empirical investigation of twice-exceptionality: Where have we been and where are we going? *Gifted Child Quarterly, 55*(1), 3-17. https://doi.org/10.1177/0016986210382575

Reis, S. M., Baum, S. M., & Burke, E. (2014). An operational definition of twice-exceptional learners: Implications and applications. *Gifted Child Quarterly, 58*(3), 217-230. https://doi.org/10.1177/0016986214547632

Roberts, J. L., & Siegle, D. (2012). Teachers as advocates: If not you, who? *Gifted Child Today, 35*(1), 58-61. https://doi.org/10.1177/1076217511427514

CHAPTER 4
Curriculum Remix: Navigating 2e Learning Landscapes

Dr Christine Ireland

A successful curriculum remix for 2e students involves accessing high levels of intellectual challenge, creative problem solving and modern technology, while keeping the best of traditional practice.

Traditional education paths for students identified as gifted have typically been separate and different to the education paths travelled by students with academic weaknesses. Exhibiting both ends of an evaluation bell curve at the same time applies to a low percentage of students. Consequently, the support required for 2e students has not easily happened within the traditional education system (King, 2022). 2e students need support inputs to strengthen their specific weaknesses while also needing the gifted education approaches associated with highly able students. For example, to motivate a gifted student teachers might include projects based on real-world issues and assessment options that reflect the students' own high-level interests.

Understanding the interests and passions of 2e students is part of a more effective modern approach. A significant 2e educational issue is the challenge of providing for students with simultaneous exceptional strengths and weaknesses. These students often exhibit:

- Asynchronous development
- Heightened overexcitabilities and sensitivities

A strictly traditional education pathway potentially can be described by an explicit teaching model rather than project-based learning model (Morret & Machado, 2017). A combination of project based learning, and explicit teaching provides a more challenging and individually relevant teaching and learning remix.

Effective extension should lead to gifted students' increased classroom engagement, improved achievement levels, and further development of their academic potential (Chowdhury, 2017; Landis & Reschly, 2013). 2e students have significant academic abilities and disabilities. Teachers therefore need highly effective professional learning in both gifted education and support education. However, Australian teacher professional learning in gifted education must be seen as under-provided (Ireland, Bowles, Nikakis, Brindle, 2020; Reid & Horváthová, 2016). Curriculum differentiation to extend highly able students is not happening adequately. Teachers' lack of time, training, resources, and the wide range of learners' ability levels in mixed ability classrooms are causal factors (Ireland, Bowles, Nikakis & Russo, 2021) in educational under-provision for 2e students.

Figure 1: Parallel Curriculum Model

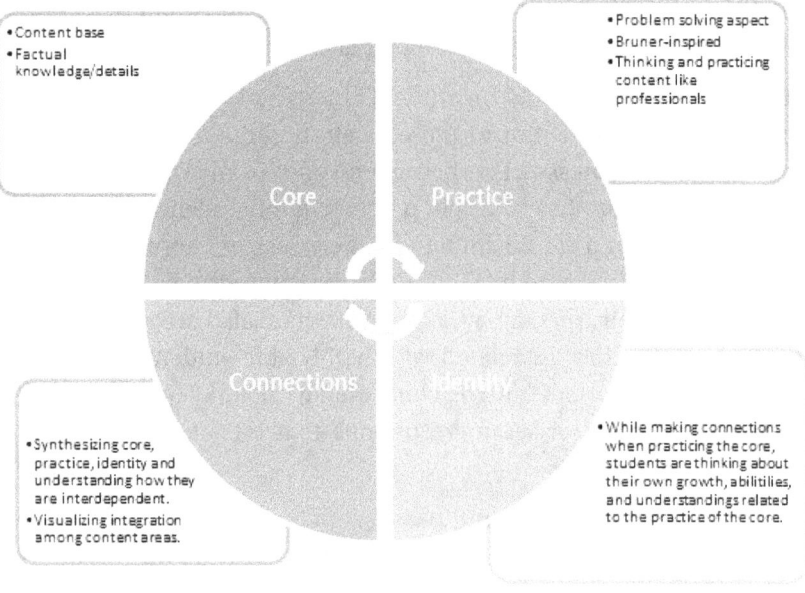

HTTPS://GIFTEDMODELS.BLOGSPOT.COM/P/PARALLEL-CURRICULUM-MODEL.HTML

Challenging the status quo

A 'standard' curricula approach for 2e students has limited success. Instead, a diversity of approaches is needed to enable their appropriate academic development. Maddocks (2020, p. 3) recommended for high ability students the "potential benefits of individualised assessment, dual differentiation, and a de-emphasis of speeded academic tasks". This is a highly individualised approach to curriculum delivery.

King (2022) similarly noted that education for 2e students needed to target individual strengths and weaknesses: "Special educators encouraged me to type at an early age, rather than continue to struggle with handwriting, and my experience in a gifted and talented program prepared me for a post-secondary education" (p. 6). The concept that the same curriculum model works for students of all ability levels and styles is not productive. Every student deserves an enriching education experience that moves them forward and engages their interest. However, too many highly able students surveyed (Ireland, Bowles, Nikakis & Brindle, 2021) felt that the education level provided in their mixed-ability classrooms was too low. This is a significant concern for Australian schools, as is the fact that student voice is rarely sought regarding this (Charteris & Smardon, 2019; Cook-Sather, 2002; Ireland, Bowles, Nikakis & Russo, 2021; Lonka & Lindblom-Ylanne, 1996).

Researchers have investigated gifted students' increasing underachievement and disengagement (Guthrie, 2020). In addition, the data from Ireland, Bowles, Nikakis, and Russo (2021), provide a window into the problem from the teachers' and students' perspective of how curriculum differentiation is being used to extend gifted and highly able students. In this research, students' survey results indicated that while they felt curriculum extension was highly important for students of high ability, it was not being achieved for them in the classroom (see Figure 2, from Ireland et al., 2020). Teachers' responses concerning extension for gifted class members echoed this sentiment. That one level of curriculum suits all students is a status quo that too often is inadequate for students of high ability, making their academic extension underachieved.

The same education for all students is neither equal, nor just (Abu, Akkanat & Gökdere, 2017; Nikakis, 2012). Given the evident problem of time stress, teachers' lack of knowledge about gifted education is highly concerning (Boettger & Reid, 2015; Laine & Tirri, 2016).

Figure 2: Comparison Teachers' and Students' Ratings of the Importance and Achievability of Curriculum Differentiation to Extend Highly Able Students (from Response Means).

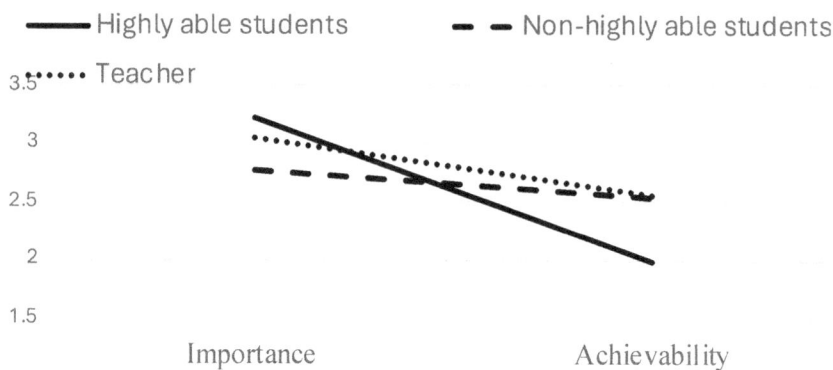

The problem of lack of extension for highly able students is reflected in a comment from one gifted student who wrote that: "It (the curriculum) can become repetitive". This student's response refers to the fact that the "weaker" students' learning needs take priority: "the curriculum is biased to children who needs more help".

Furthermore, data from participating teachers confirmed that they felt constrained by their capacity to make sure an appropriate curriculum was provided for all students in their classrooms. One teacher wrote: "Teachers are biased towards lower tiered students. Highly able students will have trouble balancing between the basics and other things. The curriculum focusses most on average students". Almost all the teachers that were surveyed agreed that schools "should offer special education services" for the highly able, and that they needed "special attention". However, it is notable that almost all disagreed that acceleration should be an extension option.

Curriculum as a palette

Any curriculum is a broad resource. It must be approached as a source of options that can build knowledge, and skills. Importantly, it must engage students' individual interests. These interests are revealed when student voice is accessed. Novak, (2024) refers to student voice as being "learner communication to influence change". Student voice can be used as a valuable input into curriculum design and delivery.

Similarly, Long (1996) contended that "The focus on the student as customer may be helpful in that the student becomes an important source of input into the educational process" (p. 280). Students need be involved in research and decisions about the need for special provision for gifted students. Long's research in 1996 referred to the generally positive reaction students had about the more highly able being given extension activities. Long stated than when asked about special classes and learning for these students, "The generally positive response contrasted with the documented hostility by adults to such provision ... of the 662 students (in the study) 87% believed that there should be special provision for faster students at secondary level" (p. 284). Further research examining how students perceive that gifted students are being extended is required.

Just as art encompasses a myriad of techniques and styles, curriculum should offer a diverse range of experiences to cater to the varied needs and interests of students. Just as not all art appeals to everyone's taste, not all educational approaches resonate equally with every learner. Modern educational philosophy emphasises the importance of personalised learning experiences that recognise and celebrate the unique strengths and interests of each student (Brown, 2020). By embracing a wide palette of teaching methods, educators can create a rich tapestry of learning opportunities that engage students and evoke a range of emotions, ultimately fostering a deeper and more meaningful educational experience (Robinson, 2015). This approach not only accommodates different learning styles but also promotes inclusivity and equity in education, ensuring that all students have the opportunity to flourish and reach their full potential (Biesta, 2018).

Depth and complexity

Depth, complexity, and creativity are essential elements of learning, especially for gifted learners. A sense of real challenge inspires and engages all learners, and teachers need to develop activities that stimulate and inspire students. Education that is too easy or the 'same old same old' is not useful for gifted students. Creativity is also fundamental to all positive learning achievement (Leikin & Sriraman, 2022). A negative attitude to the need for extension education for the gifted may very well be a foundational cause for some highly able students' decreasing achievement rates (Macy, 2017; Mullen & Jung, 2019; Russell, 2018).

On a positive note, the Australian Curriculum Assessment and Reporting Authority (ACARA) (2021) refers to Australian teachers being able to adapt the Australian Curriculum to suit the level of learning of highly able students: "(the) gifted and talented (receive) a curriculum that supports all students to achieve their full potential". However, this clearly indicates that significant training for teachers in gifted education would be required to adequately deliverer these adaptations for academically able students. ACARA (2021) has provided videos and associated resources that address diversity of ability in the classroom.

Australian teachers attempt to adapt their curricular for the gifted (Jolly & Robins, 2021). The difficulty of adequate provision for the gifted is not limited to Australia and is experienced internationally (Clark & Roberts, 2018). Vreys, Ndungbogun, Kieboom, and Venderickx (2018) noted that this was a problem in Belgium. Vreys et. al., contended that in Belgium the "lack of knowledge of effective educational interventions" was part of the basis of this problem. Vreys also emphasised that a lack of appropriate teacher training leads to misconceptions about gifted students leading to "well-intentioned but ineffective interventions" (p. 3).

Below is an example of ways in which complexity and depth can be added to current Australian Curriculum content, while still scaffolding the needs of diverse learners.

Subject area	Primary curriculum	Secondary curriculum
English	Analyse complex texts and write original stories. Example: Comparing and contrasting characters in literature. Draft the same story from 3 perspectives, the main character, the main villain, and the environment or setting.	Analyse complex texts and author analytical essays. Example: Conducting literary analysis of Shakespearean sonnets. Create innovative words like Shakespeare did, create new phrases and terminology to adequately express the emotions and ideas, create a glossary of terms, then construct a sonnet, play or prose using the new terminology.
Maths	Explore advanced math concepts like geometry. Example: Investigating geometric shapes and their properties, conducting investigations to demonstrate proofs.	Explore advanced math concepts like calculus. Example: Solving differential equations and optimisation problems. Look at real world complex maths issues, create or prove a formula, to increase financial security into the future. Encourage students to work on problem solving and physical maths activities that are meaningful and relevant.
Science	Conduct simple experiments and explore basic scientific concepts. Example: Exploring the properties of magnets, create the smallest and strongest electromagnet, investigate the use for hover boards and cars, using the earth's magnetic field, or a new road surface.	Conduct complex experiments and analyse data. Example: Investigating genetic inheritance patterns in biology. Problem solves a real-world issue and develops and test hypothesis, such as the plastic problem worldwide, or local impact of modernisation, on a species native to your area. Link in with the CSIRO scientists in schools' programs to deepen understanding.

Subject area	Primary curriculum	Secondary curriculum
Humanities	Learn about historical events through storytelling and interactive activities. Example: Creating a timeline of noteworthy events. Encourage social experiments of living history such as medieval fairs, and school through the ages.	Engage in critical analysis of historical events and primary sources. Example: Debating the causes of World War II. Investigate the 'now' and develop ideas of how we can be good ancestors to future generations. What will the people of 2124, say about us?
Art	Experiment with different art mediums and techniques. Example: Creating collages using various materials. Create living art, incorporating plants into living sculptures for the school environment.	Explore art history and theory and create original artworks. Example: Analysing the symbolism in surrealist paintings. Invite artists to come to the school and dig deep into galleries and exhibitions. Look at indigenous artists and techniques as well as traditional eastern and western art.
Music	Sing simple songs and explore basic musical concepts. Example: Use a stepped process to create your own music, using a variety of percussion and voice sounds. Implement digital editing to create music, experience live music and listen to and explore music from other cultures, and times.	Study music theory and perform complex pieces. Example: Analysing the structure and harmony of classical compositions. Create emotional music, music to help you sleep and study. Look at the idea of 'new classical' what does that look like and mean. Have we lost the art of making music in a digital age?

Analysing how to challenge the gifted while captivating their imagination is a common goal among teachers. Teachers understand that unchallenging work for students leads to boredom and disengagement. Van Tassel-Baska and MacFarlane (2008) explained that the priority for advanced learning for the highly able as: "Gifted learners at secondary levels appear to benefit from advanced instruction in science, consistent with their levels of functioning in the subject, but beyond the typical level of science offered by the school" (p. 589). Without extension highly able students' academic results decline (Ritchotte, Rubenstein & Murry, 2015 and Figures 3 and 4). In addition, McCoach and Siegle (2008) contended that the effects of underachievement on these students may be very long-lasting.

Renzulli (2021) provided an excellent teacher resource regarding the development of creative productive giftedness. Renzulli (2021) noted the importance behind challenging and inspiring gifted students as "Our history and culture can be charted to a large extent by the creative contributions of the world's most gifted and talented individuals" (p. 13). He explains that "educators (must) integrate applied and created knowledge with advanced content" (p.23) and that learners are increasingly dealing with real life problems and using advanced and evolving technologies.

Figure 3: PISA Science and Mathematics Scores Declining

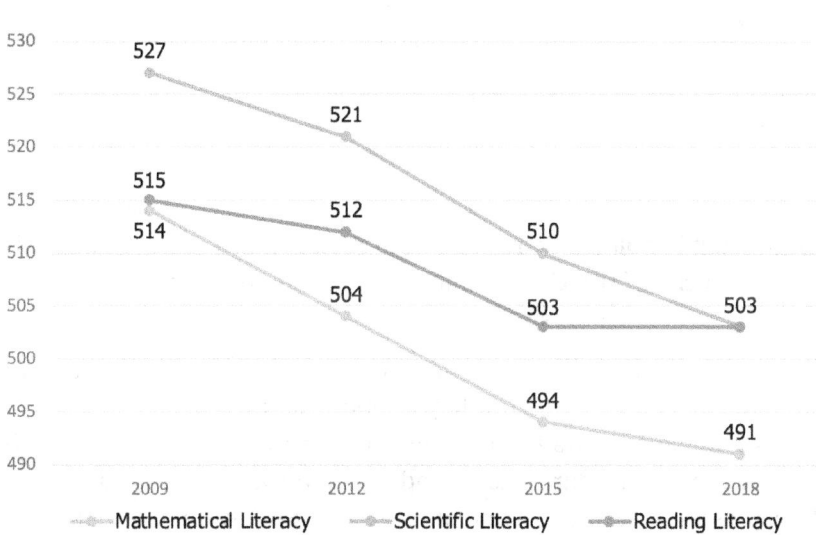

ACARA (2015) stated that gifted and talented students are suited to more difficult and challenging work than other students at the chronological level of their study. ACARA has also contended that the Australian Curriculum can be adapted so that students' learning can be linked more closely to their capability level. Consequently, the issue of highly able students'

underachievement is a highly serious dilemma, evident in more than just declining PISA (see Figure 3) and TIMSS' results 2009-2018 (Buckingham, 2016; Masters, 2015; Masters, 2016). It is an issue that is relevant to current Australian education sectors.

Figure 4: NAPLAN New South Wales 2011–2017

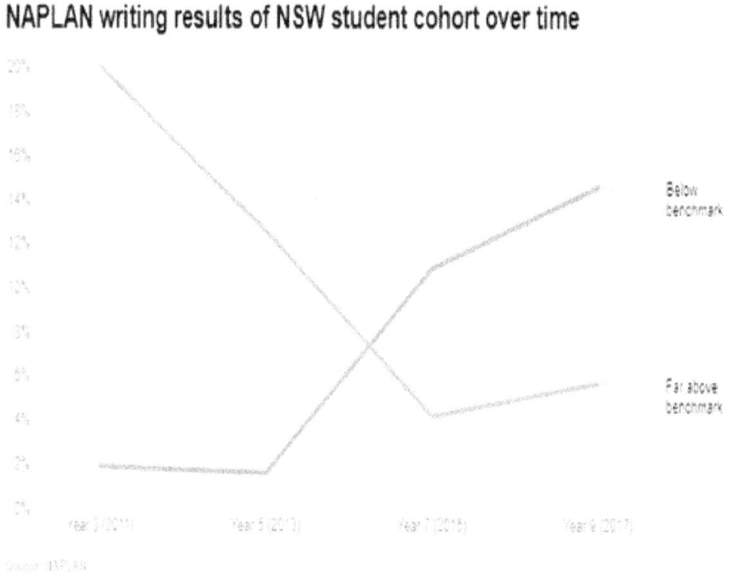

NAPLAN writing results of NSW student cohort over time

Similarly, highly able students' NAPLAN results (see Figure 4) showed a significant decline (The Conversation, 2017). The following results (NSW 2011-2018) were reflected similarly across Australia.

In particular, students surveyed by Ireland et al. (2021) felt that the curriculum as presented to the highly able was too easy for them, that weaker students were the teachers' priority, and that teachers lacked the time, capacity, and resources to extend the highly able. Surveyed students (n19) expressed that their curriculum learning level was being set too low. These problems are reflected in a comment from one student (identified by the teacher as highly able) who wrote that "Because they understand and know what is being taught... it can become repetitive". One student even outlined one of the extension obstacles for highly able students as: "Simple assignments and worksheets they already know how and what to do in them and find it extremely easy". It would seem then that the students, regardless of ability level are aware that there is an extension problem for the highly able, and what might be causing it. Clearly, teachers do well when they challenge gifted students and increase their awareness of how these students are thinking.

Gifted students undoubtedly need critical thinking and deep learning. That teachers work hard and are time poor is understood within all aspects of education. The surveyed students made several astute comments such as "the teacher will find it hard to teach two levels at once". Students surveyed also understood the attraction for many teachers for a 'one size fits all' curriculum. One student noted: "the teacher usually picks tasks that are suitable to everyone" and that highly able students were therefore "not able to do what their level is at school". Unfortunately, some responses referred to highly able students as simply not being identified by teachers as students who needed to be challenged.

Therefore, an adequate breadth of identification of these students is required. All aspects of giftedness including creative and physical learning needs to be addressed (Uçara & Sungurb, 2018). Learning disabilities should not impede this identification process. Teachers must become aware of how their understanding of how gifted students feel about the extension they receive in the classroom. Teachers' and students' perceptions of the obstacles to providing extension for the highly able is a critical factor to examine. When asked what obstacles they perceived in providing extension for their highly able students teachers' (and students') responses included: teachers' limited time, resources, and training. Teachers need support in these areas if they are to inspire students to fully develop their own skills and fields of interest.

Passion projects and individualised challenges

To encourage students to develop their own passions while achieving curriculum goals allows them to develop educationally in an authentic and exciting way. To achieve this a teacher models, and expects from the learner, a deep level of inquiry into issues, skills and knowledge bases. A broad range of field experts and resources are drawn upon.

Teachers attempt to develop individualised programs for their students. In Ireland et al. (2021) teachers (n28) unanimously indicated that highly able students needed special attention to be able to develop their talents, and 22 out of 28 agreed that schools should be providing this. However, the majority (n23) felt that separating students into highly able and other groups increases the labelling of children as strong, weak, good, less-good etc. Most teachers (n21) disagreed that highly able students were currently already favoured in schools and did not feel that they were becoming vain or egotistical (n23). Furthermore, the majority of teachers surveyed felt that special programs for the highly able would not be considered "elitism", and that these students would not become "vain or egotistical" if they received special attention. It is also significant that mixed-ability classes provide the greatest challenge for teachers (Johnson, 2000; McCoach & Siegle, 2008; Siegle & McCoach, 2018; Suprayogi, Valcke & Godwin, 2017; Watters & Diezmann, 2003). This makes providing individualised challenges more difficult.

Marsili, Dell'Anna and Pellegrini (2023) noted that teaching gifted students in inclusive mixed-ability classes may have positive social outcomes, but it may also lead to frustration and disengagement for the highly able. Ronksley-Pavia and Neuman (2020) felt that re-engaging gifted learners required a high level of understanding of each gifted student's individual interest profile to personalise pedagogical approaches. Similarly, it was suggested by Ng (2018, p. iii) that "recognition of learning strengths, alongside provision for learning difficulties" were essential components in solving the problem of student disengagement. Knowing the student well is repeatedly offered as the first step to solving the problem. In addition, authors such as Robinson, Shore and Enerson (2021) regarding the 2e learning landscape suggest to "overtly teach coping strategies and to use individually adapted assessments". They recommend that education planning requires teams including external professionals, and that families and schools must be included in relevant discussions.

Balancing challenge and support

An overload of work does not automatically produce a significant increase in learning outcomes or achievement for highly able students. Instead, by tailoring the challenges to be 'just beyond' a student's level encourages them to stretch just a little further to achieve the task, utilising Vygotsky (1978) Zone of proximal development. Their consistent references to unchallenging curricula are not solved by more 'busy work'. For 2e students the balance between challenge and support must be carefully planned.

Without this balanced provision, students will become stressed and discouraged.

The data from Ireland et al. (2001) referred to difficulties that stress places on gifted students within the education system. The extra work they are given as part of their 'extension' by some teachers was described as significantly worrying and burdensome. Several high ability students reported if they finished the general classwork quickly, being automatically expected to assist academically weaker students was considered normal and contributed significantly to the stress they felt about school.

Becoming a teacher for gifted students comes with unique challenges and opportunities, particularly regarding mental wellbeing. While these students possess exceptional abilities, they also face heightened expectations, social pressures, and sometimes feelings of isolation due to their differences. As educators, it is crucial to foster an environment that supports their intellectual growth while also prioritising their emotional and psychological needs.

Research by Gallagher and Gallagher (2017) emphasises the importance of creating a safe and inclusive classroom environment where gifted students feel understood, valued, and supported. This involves implementing strategies for stress management, promoting resilience, and providing access to counselling or mental health resources when needed (Kerr, 2017). Additionally, collaborative partnerships between teachers, parents, and mental health professionals can play a pivotal role in addressing the multifaceted needs of gifted students (Neihart, Reis, Robinson & Moon, 2002). By prioritising the academic needs of gifted and 2e students educators will also benefit the mental wellbeing of gifted students. In this way educators can help cultivate their full potential and pave the way for lifelong success and fulfillment. As educators catering for 2e students our mantra should be different not more.

Incorporating interests and strengths

Individualising the learning for students is not about aiming to teach a different lesson to every student, each lesson. It is also not about assuming that highly able students need separate lessons for every subject. It is about providing a curriculum plan that achieves the learning goals within the curriculum while developing a 2e students' own interests and challenges.

Doing this while providing the required extra support to assist with areas of academic weakness are also essential. This balance requires:

- Whole school support and understanding of 2e needs
- Relevant 2e resourcing and professional learning

Current Australian research indicates that 2e learners thrive when given the opportunity to explore topics of personal interest and engage in self-directed learning. According to Reis and McCoach (2000), allowing 2e students to pursue areas of passion can unlock their full potential and enhance their academic achievement. By incorporating choice into the curriculum, educators can automatically add the depth and complexity that these students require to excel. This approach aligns with the principles of personalised learning, which emphasises student autonomy, agency, and intrinsic motivation (Bray & McClaskey, 2015). When 2e learners are empowered to research, study, and focus on topics that resonate with their unique interests and talents, they are more likely to demonstrate high levels of engagement, creativity, and critical thinking (Robinson & Noble, 2016). Moreover, providing opportunities for self-directed learning enables 2e students to develop essential skills such as problem-solving, self-regulation, and perseverance, which are vital for success in both academic and real-world contexts (Mishra & Koehler, 2006). By embracing a student-centred approach that prioritises choice and autonomy, educators can create inclusive learning environments where 2e learners can thrive and reach their full potential.

Educators need to be aware that giftedness is not defined as being automatically high performing across all domains. The factor of teachers' limited time to achieve extension for highly able students was described by students (as well as teachers) as one of the most significant problems. This is a common theme mentioned by educators: Bahar, Kaya and Bahar (2016); Coleman & Cross (2021). Another frequently identified problem according to the surveyed teachers and students according to Ireland et al. (2021) was the difficulty teachers had providing for the breadth of ability levels in the classrooms. Most of the students felt that teachers were not providing an advanced curriculum for the highly able because weaker academic ability students were their priority. One student wrote: "Teachers are biased towards lower tiered students …the curriculum focusses most on average students". One student felt that the teaching focus was on "Other children which aren't as capable as them". Several students were also aware that the highly able students were not getting education at the level they required because of this problem. Another student highlighted "Teachers being too focused on other children and then the highly able don't get enough attention". One student wrote: "There isn't enough time for people to teach them". Another wrote stating a problem for teachers providing for the needs of these students was "the amount of time it takes to organise".

While students and teachers recognised the burden of simultaneous support and extension of 2e students, it does not alleviate the injustice of daily inappropriate classwork for these students. Many of the highly able students' survey responses about obstacles to receiving appropriate levels of curriculum differentiation recognise that the education system, not the teachers, was to blame. Teachers and students agreed that lack of appropriate teacher training caused some teachers' inability to provide for these gifted students. Teachers and students were also in agreement that the lack of appropriate resources was another obstacle to high ability students being adequately educated.

Kanevsky (2011) noted that highly able students most wanted to be able to work simply at their own pace, to select a complex topic within the curriculum offerings (as well as from extra-curricular topics) and to choose the students to work with. This applies to 2e students as well. Again, training in gifted and support education would make this clear. From this sort of professional learning, 2e students would make sophisticated interconnections among the ideas offered. Undergraduate training must become a priority for all institutes of teacher training. Post-graduate training is also needed as professional development, but, as one teacher put it, in a "coordinated" way. Coordination of extension and support training is a priority.

In summary, to balance challenge and support in order to address 2e students' strengths and weaknesses:

- Have a high level of understanding of the student's academic capacities.
- Encourage students to express their areas of talent and interest.
- Provide assessment options that include open-ended project work.
- Link the curriculum content to current real-world issues and technology.

- Seek student input within the design and evaluation phase of each unit.
- Ensure that teachers are professionally developed in both support and extension.

Embracing the remix

A successful curriculum re-mix for a gifted learner, as for any learner, calls for them to demonstrate the required learning of the curriculum in a way that is both challenging and uniquely interesting for them. This can become a life-long learning model for students as they approach each new task from a point of view that is unique to their own developing ability levels and interests. Rennie, Venville and Wallace (2018) wrote about how to link individual interests to the curriculum as part of contextual, multidisciplinary issue-based learning. Rennie et al. (2018, p. 103) stated that "While big ideas require robust technical knowledge, invariably they also incorporate the social, cultural, and political and as such are used to help students become better informed, better connected and better able to take appropriate action on the problems of their world". Rennie et al. (2018) suggested options for students could include:

- Select a topic that is related to a big idea in the curriculum.
- Identify the relevant skills concerning the student's need.
- Identify the issues that are of immediate concern to students locally and globally.
- Elicit the student's current understandings to illuminate the gaps.
- Acknowledge student's viewpoints to ensure that they can feel personally involved.
- Determine how this topic will assist real world understanding.
- Determine the pedagogical strategies to achieve these curriculum goals.
- Provide practical problems for students to solve.
- Involve the local community.

Clearly, it is important to establish the learning levels and interests of each student. Effective communication between each student, their teachers and families are the key to this. Recognising high potential is a powerful motivational force for all stakeholders. Taking inspiration from schools that are demonstrating effective curriculum differentiation programs is a further way to develop programs suitable for other educators. The program ASPIRE (Achieving Specific Personal Inspiration with Real Enrichment) developed by a school in Texas (Corpus Christ, St Ives is an exemplar of this). The ASPIRE program focuses on design thinking, philosophical questions, and areas of interest for selected students. Sharing successful programs, including the commonly known Bloom's Taxonomy, is an essential element within effective differentiated education.

Some 2e students clearly are learning within excellent curriculum models, while others are still under-provided for. King (2022, p.2) summed this up as "supports related to disability diagnosis and enrichment activities associated with gifted education are often disjointed or withheld entirely, resulting in suboptimal outcomes for this population".

However, many educators have made substantial improvements in this area. For example, Australia's STEM program has positively impacted science, technology and mathematics domains significantly. Many schools provide diverse and valuable extra-curricular activities and access to experts within the community. Van Tassel-Baska and MacFarlane (2008) explained that "gifted learners at secondary levels profit from real-world internships in laboratories, hospitals, and other research settings that allow them to see and participate in science being done professionally" (p. 589). 2e education is drawing teachers, students and families towards a far richer educational experience that will have life-long advantages for individuals, and for the broader community.

 **KEY TAKEAWAYS**

- **Individualised curriculum for 2e students:** A successful curriculum remix for 2e students involves combining traditional and innovative approaches, such as explicit teaching with project-based learning. This balance addresses both strengths and challenges while fostering creativity, critical thinking, and real-world problem-solving.

- **Challenges of curriculum differentiation:** Traditional education systems often fail to meet the dual needs of 2e students due to a lack of teacher training, resources, and time. These systemic issues hinder the implementation of curriculum differentiation, leaving both gifted abilities and disabilities insufficiently supported.

- **Student voice in curriculum design:** Incorporating student voice into curriculum planning is vital for engaging 2e students. Understanding their interests, passions, and individual learning needs enhances educational experiences and ensures curriculum delivery is relevant and challenging.

- **Importance of professional development:** Teachers require targeted professional development in both gifted education and support education to effectively meet the needs of 2e learners. Lack of teacher training in this area is a global issue, leading to underachievement and disengagement among highly able students.

- **Balancing challenge and support:** For 2e students, the balance between challenge and support is crucial. This includes tailored learning experiences that stretch their abilities without overloading them, while also addressing their areas of need. Linking curriculum content to real-world issues and encouraging self-directed learning are effective strategies.

Chapter references

Abu, R. B., Akkanat, C., & Gökdere, M. (2017). Supporting gifted students with learning disabilities: Research and practice. *Journal of Advanced Academics, 28*(3), 225–241. https://doi.org/10.1177/1932202X17711441

Australian Curriculum, Assessment and Reporting Authority (ACARA). (2021). Supporting gifted and talented students. Retrieved from https://www.acara.edu.au

Biesta, G. (2018). What is the educational task? *Educational Theory, 68*(4-5), 391–406. https://doi.org/10.1111/edth.12311

Boettger, H., & Reid, E. (2015). Gifted education in various countries of Europe. *Slavonic Pedagogical Studies Journal, 4*(2), 158–171.

Brown, A. L. (2020). Personalised learning: The role of student agency in curriculum design. *Journal of Curriculum Studies, 52*(3), 337–354. https://doi.org/10.1080/00220272.2020.1773492

Charteris, J., & Smardon, D. (2019). Student voice in learning: Instrumentalism and tokenism or opportunity for altering the status quo? *Journal of Educational Change, 20*(4), 387–411.

Chowdhury, R. A. (2017). Addressing the needs of gifted students: Insights into curriculum differentiation. *Gifted Education International, 33*(2), 115–130. https://doi.org/10.1177/0261429417708878

Clark, B., & Roberts, J. L. (2018). Building a system of support for classroom teachers working with gifted students. *Teaching Exceptional Children, 50*(4), 265–273.

Cook-Sather, A. (2002). Authorizing students' perspectives: Toward trust, dialogue, and change in education. *Educational Researcher, 31*(4), 3–14.

Ireland, C., Bowles, T., Nikakis, C., & Brindle, R. (2020). Understanding gifted education in Australian schools: Teachers' perspectives on differentiation. *Australasian Journal of Gifted Education, 29*(1), 5–18.

Ireland, M., Bowles, T., Nikakis, C., & Russo, J. (2021). Extending gifted learners in mixed-ability classrooms: Insights from Australian students and teachers. *Australasian Journal of Gifted Education, 30*(1), 29–41. https://doi.org/10.21505/ajge.2021.0003

Jolly, J. L., & Robins, J. H. (2021). History and context of gifted education. In *Handbook of Giftedness and Talent Development* (pp. 17–30). Springer.

King, J. (2022). Supporting twice-exceptional students: Educational interventions and best practices. *Twice Exceptional Education Quarterly, 15*(2), 1–10.

Laine, S., & Tirri, K. (2016). How Finnish elementary school teachers meet the needs of their gifted students. *High Ability Studies, 27*(2), 149–164.

Landis, R. N., & Reschly, A. L. (2013). Reexamining gifted underachievement and dropout through the lens of student engagement. *Journal for the Education of the Gifted, 36*(2), 220–249.

Leikin, R., & Sriraman, B. (2022). *Creativity and giftedness: Advances in mathematics education*. Springer.

Lonka, K., & Lindblom-Ylanne, S. (1996). Epistemologies, conceptions of learning, and studypractices in medicine and psychology. *Higher Education, 31*(1), 5–24.

Macy, M. (2017). *Teaching gifted learners in today's preschool and primary classrooms*. Free Spirit Publishing.

Maddocks, D. L. S. (2020). Effective curriculum adaptations for gifted learners. *Gifted Child Today, 43*(3), 157–163. https://doi.org/10.1177/1076217520908576

Mullen, C. A., & Jung, J. (2019). *Gifted education in STEM disciplines: Critical perspectives on talent development*. Routledge.

Morret, D., & Machado, C. (2017). Blending traditional and project-based learning for twice-exceptional students. *Educational Strategies Quarterly, 22*(4), 35–48.

Nikakis, S. (2012). Differentiating the curriculum: A case study in secondary education. *Australasian Journal of Gifted Education, 21*(2), 34–45

Reid, E., & Horváthová, B. (2016). Teacher training programs for gifted education with focus on sustainability. *Journal of Teacher Education for Sustainability*, 18(2), 66–74.

Rennie, L. J., Venville, G. J., & Wallace, J. (2018). Designing curriculum for authentic learning: STEM approaches. *Australian Journal of Education, 62*(2), 95–112. https://doi.org/10.1177/0004944118774991

Robinson, K. (2015). *Creative schools: The grassroots revolution that's transforming education.* Penguin Books.

Robinson, K., & Noble, T. (2016). Personalized learning pathways for twice-exceptional students. Gifted Education International, 32(3), 225–239. https://doi.org/10.1177/0261429416645119

Russell, J. L. (2018). High school teachers' perceptions of giftedness, gifted education, and talent development. *Journal for the Education of the Gifted, 41*(4), 242–263.

Van Tassel-Baska, J., & MacFarlane, B. A. (2008). Science curriculum extensions for gifted learners: Real-world learning. *Gifted Child Quarterly, 52*(4), 585–594. https://doi.org/10.1177/0016986208323482

Vreys, C., Ndungbogun, E., Kieboom, T., & Venderickx, K. (2018). Educating gifted learners in Belgium: A focus on teacher training and intervention strategies. *Gifted and Talented International, 33*(1-2), 3–16. https://doi.org/10.1080/15332276.2018.1429295

CHAPTER 5
Gifted Yet Hindered – Explaining Impaired Cognitive Functions

Catherine Cross

For better or worse, teachers play a vital role in the lives of their students. Their knowledge of cognitive and social development, educational theories and curriculum expertise, position them to impact the lives of young people daily. As the demands faced by students are intensifying, affective, academic and neurological support, is becoming a combined focus for educators to proactively cater for. Despite this, many teachers do not feel equipped to serve each pupil accordingly, particularly teachers of twice-exceptional (2e) students. Misunderstandings regarding the neurological challenges faced by 2e individuals has given rise to adverse perceptions of this cohort with many teachers struggling to grasp the permanence of a neurological deficit in contrast with the student's naturally high capabilities (Atkins, 2020; Lucas & Soares, 2013; National Association for Gifted and Talented Children, 2021; Peterson, 2016).

Taming the tongue

Meet Asha. A cheerful, funny girl with boundless energy, hundreds of thoughts per minute, a remarkable imagination and an active problem-solver, when she can stay focused! She's the type who will start talking about the best way to fix a tap then, before you know it, has detoured off on a tangent about miming in the mirror and the questionable poem choice at last week's school assembly. Then finally she concludes with her speculation that possums are devouring the local magnolias. Her friends have learned to expect conversation interjections and tangents, but Asha's chatter also reveals sensitivities, high social-intelligence, and surprisingly mature insights. Yet, when you think she's finally settled and focused, she will whiz out a sticky-note jotting down an idea or solution, then bounding off again to see what everyone else is doing. Asha may appear an industrious social butterfly, but her curious, creative, distractable mind works overtime. For her, every day feels like a marathon as she anxiously manages the expectations of a neurotypical world, with a neurodivergent brain. Despite her capable intellect, attention deficit hyperactivity disorder has impaired her executive functions, and while they cannot be 'fixed' – they can be understood and managed.

What are executive functions?

Executive Function is an umbrella term used to describe cognitive processes; planning, working memory, attention, inhibition, self-monitoring, self-regulation, initiation, and emotional regulation. These mental processes are interconnected and synchronised allowing people to focus, organise, remember instructions, pay attention and manage multiple tasks.

To enable these functions to work successfully, the brain must utilise the following::

- **Working memory** directs the ability to retain and manipulate pieces of information over a short time frame.
- **Mental flexibility** sustains or shifts attention in response to pressures or applying different rules in different settings.
- **Self-control** assists in prioritising, resists impulsive actions, interjections or responses.

(Brown, 2005; The President and Fellows of Harvard College, 2024; Oxford Dictionary, 2024).

Previous research by psychologist Micheal Posner (1975) proposed that a separate branch of executive functions exists for focus, attention and cognitive control. Consensus with his findings has consistently emerged since, and now there are over 30 varying constructs all generated to explain 'executive function' (Goldstein et. al., 2014). Further research then discovered that for many neurodivergent individuals, cognitive functions don't perform as effectively as they do in a neurotypical brain. Thomas E. Brown, professor of Psychiatry and Neuroscience at the University of California, developed a model to visually demonstrate the complexities of the brain's cognitive management system (Brown Clinic for Attention & Related Disorders, 2024). His findings shed light on persons diagnosed as neurodivergent and explained how these functions were naturally impaired.

Figure 1: Brown Model of Executive Functions Impaired in ADHD

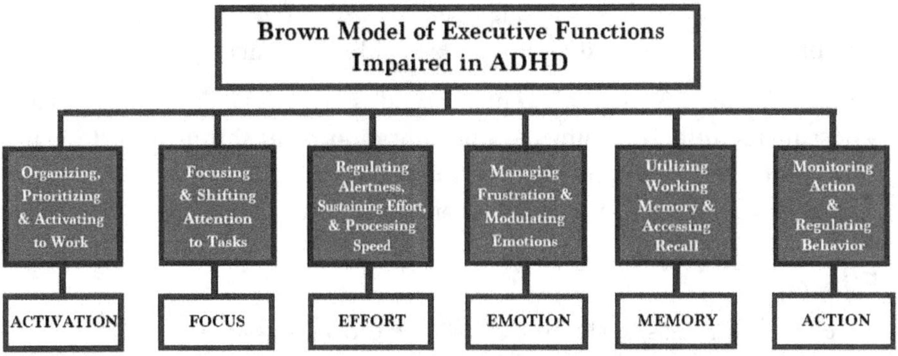

```
                    Brown Model of Executive Functions
                           Impaired in ADHD

  Organizing,    Focusing    Regulating    Managing     Utilizing    Monitoring
  Prioritizing   & Shifting  Alertness,    Frustration  Working      Action
  & Activating   Attention   Sustaining    & Modulating Memory &     & Regulating
  to Work        to Tasks    Effort,       Emotions     Accessing    Behavior
                             & Processing               Recall
                             Speed

  ACTIVATION     FOCUS       EFFORT        EMOTION      MEMORY       ACTION
```

(BROWN MODEL OF EXECUTIVE FUNCTIONS, 2005).

Although viewed as six separate functions, all are intertwined, rapidly and unconsciously working together and increasing in complexity as the brain matures. However, for many 2e students, they face difficulty in the development and use of these functions when compared with their same aged neurotypical peers.

Activation

Organising tasks, materials, time management, task prioritisation, and commencing tasks.

Difficulties with procrastination, motivation and attention.

Students may put off beginning the task, even one they recognise as very important, until the last minute. They cannot get themselves started until they perceive the task as an acute emergency.

Focus

Focusing, sustaining focus, and shifting focus from task to task.

Struggling to sustain focus may present as zoning-in and zoning-out, physical movement, endless chatter or looking around the room.

Distractions are both environmental and internal, such as personal thoughts, concerns, overwhelm, or imagination.

Focus on reading poses difficulties for many. Words are generally understood as they are read, but often may be read repeatedly for the meaning to be fully grasped and remembered.

2e students with slow processing speed benefit from task forewarning so they have time to collect their thoughts to aid engagement.

Research indicates that students should start working on key tasks/assessments in the mornings as concentration fades throughout the day. Some students have indicated that they are distracted not only by things going on around them, but also by their own thoughts.

Effort

Regulating alertness, sustaining effort, and processing speed.

Performs short-term projects well, difficulty with sustained effort over longer periods of time.

Completing tasks on time, especially when they require handwriting, is hard as they struggle to get their knowledge in appropriate written form on the page. As verbal skills are their strength, oral presentations, recoding or having a scribe, ease the amount of effort, stress and anxiety attributed to task completion.

Many also experience chronic insomnia and sleep deprivation. Often, they can't stop or turn-off the constant chatter in their minds especially as they begin to unwind and process their thoughts. Over thinking social-emotional issues, academic pressures, friendships and busy week schedules fuel their evening 'alertness'. When they finally sleep, many have trouble with the quality of sleep and don't get the required hours needed, thus, waking fatigued.

Intense Emotions

Emotions are experienced very intensely. Heightened feelings of passion, frustration, enthusiasm, anger, rejection, or excitement.

Impulsive emotional reactions include:

- Calling out answers before the question is complete.
- Speaking out of turn.
- Interrupting other speakers.
- Standing, swaying, fidgeting or moving when they need to sit still.
- Giving in to distraction.
- Engaging in unsafe behaviour.
- Experiencing reduced emotional regulation.
- Succumbing to significantly larger impulses to achieve a release of dopamine. e.g. spending money, binge eating, or experimenting with substances.

Difficulty with emotional regulation; the highs are high, and the lows are low. Often leading to a sense of overwhelm and a hyper focus on negative emotions.

Their central nervous system operates in a state of high anxiety which accumulates and transfers into feelings of overwhelm, stress, and in some cases, becomes depression.

Rejection sensitivity, especially if they interpret or perceive others are displeased with them.

Memory

Utilising working memory and accessing recall.

Some students have an exceptional memory for things that happened long ago, however, their short working memory impacts daily life, e.g. struggling to recall where they just put something, or what they were about to do.

Frustrations occur over simple tasks as they cannot hold many verbal instructions and can have a poor memory for the details they have recently learned and read. Stress rises when they need to make important decisions without time to process or retrieve the information.

Action

Monitoring and regulating self-action.

Chronic problems with regulating their actions. They can be too impulsive in what they say or do, the way they think, and jump to inaccurate conclusions. For example uncontrollable chatter, interrupting other speakers or speaking out of turn, standing, swaying, fidgeting or moving when they need to sit still and giving into distractions.

Some struggle to monitor the context in which they are interacting, failing to notice when other people are puzzled, hurt or annoyed by what they have just said or done.

Difficulty in regulating the pace of their actions, in slowing self and/or speeding up as needed for specific tasks.

The 2e 'Top Four' and Best Practice

Autism Spectrum Disorder	
Generalised Function Impairments	**Best Teaching Practice**
- **Cognitive flexibility:** struggles to switch between or divide two separate concepts and think about them from different perspectives. - **Action:** difficulties monitoring and regulating self-action and control over distractions. - **Activation:** poor organisation of items, time, or priorities. - **Focus:** struggles to focus and sustain focus. When hyper-focused they may struggle to then shift focus to another task. - **Effort:** regulating alertness, sustaining effort and processing speed are physically exhausting. - **Working memory:** difficulty to mentally hold information and access recall that is needed for learning, everyday functions, or immediate use.	- Limit sensory overload. - Use incentives to increase student engagement. - Utilise 'Applied Behaviour Analysis' therapy. - Provide immediate feedback, correction and praise. - Focus on reading and comprehension development. - Encourage communication that is friendly, polite and clear. - Practice social skills through role play, games or practical interactions as a whole class, pairs or inter-class activities. - Large visual routines and instructions displayed in a prominent area. - Pre-warn students if the routine will change. - Utilise social stories. - Encourage communication and social skill support services or therapies. (Honeybourne, 2018; Leonard, 2024)

Attention Deficit Disorder with/without Hyperactivity	
Generalised Function Impairments	**Best Teaching Practice**
- **Activation:** organising and prioritising tasks and materials, estimating time for tasks, time blindness when focused on a task, difficulty starting a task if motivation is low. - **Focus:** difficulty focusing, sustaining focus, and shifting focus from task to task. - **Effort:** challenges regulating alertness, sustaining effort, and the additional energy required due to slow processing speed. - **Intense emotions:** heightened feelings of passion, love, frustration, enthusiasm, anger, rejection, or excitement. - **Memory:** difficulty to mentally hold information and access recall that is needed for learning, everyday functions, or immediate use. - **Action:** difficulty monitoring and regulating behaviour, impulses, or self-control. The inability to ignore or disengage from distractions, and modulate the anxiety generated by the setting.	- Give short, clear, repeated information in chunks. - Reduce the volume of unnecessary 'fluff' by giving the essential key learnings only. - Allow time to process, practice and consolidate the learning before moving the student onto something new. - Help the student get their thoughts from their *head-to-the-page*. - Display visual routines and time frames for each portion of the task to be completed. - Utilise IT for reading, spelling and recording information e.g. talk to text, immersive reader, audio books. - Roam the room so redirection and focus prompting can be discreet. - Avoid repeatedly calling out the student's name to reengage them as has a negative connotation, translating as, 'you are always in trouble'. - Remove distractions and clutter from worktables and benches. Reduce noise. (ADHD Foundation, 2021; Honeybourne, 2018)

Dyslexia	
Generalised Function Impairments	**Best Teaching Practice**
• **Memory:** short working memory when trying to recall information that impacts decoding, sequencing events, remembering/naming letters, numbers and colours and processing information. – Difficulty mentally holding information and accessing learning details, or general recall for everyday functions, or immediate use. • **Activation:** difficulty with organisation, prioritisation of the time, remembering date and deadlines. • **Action:** difficulty monitoring and regulating behaviour. Often displaying the inability to ignore or disengage from distractions. • **Focus:** difficulty shifting focus from task-to-task without disengaging. • **Effort:** challenges maintaining effort when decoding, verbal processing and then understanding the information.	• Re-training the auditory and visual systems to process sounds and letters (accurately). This prepares the brain for new learning and the retention of reading/spelling skills. • Deliver key content, instructions, and outputs, in a manner that aligns with the student's strengths. • Kinesthetics approaches using tactile equipment enables the student to tangibly make a connection between the sound and letter. • Extra time allowance for task completion. Remove time restrictions for assessments and tests. • Responding verbally either by recording their understanding/answers or having a scribe write their responses/answers verbatim. • The teacher should provide a summary of key content, skeleton outlines of requirements, note taking prompts, concept maps and offering digital apps. (Australian Online Courses, 2024; Baumer, 2021)

Dysgraphia	
Generalised Function Impairments	**Best Teaching Practice**
• **Memory:** difficulty holding and manipulating information that relates to decoding, sequencing events, remembering/naming letters, numbers and colours and processing information. – Difficulty mentally holding information and accessing learning details, or general recall for everyday functions, or immediate use. • **Activation:** difficulty with organisation, prioritisation of the time, remembering date and deadlines. Goal setting, organising, shifting, working memory, and self-checking/self-monitoring. • **Effort:** challenges maintaining effort when decoding, verbal processing and then understanding the information. Language processing skills are compromised.	• Explicit interventions in phonics, spelling conventions, morphology, syntax and grammar, sentence and paragraph composition. • Short, achievable goals for anything handwritten. • Extra time to complete written tasks. • Utilising assistive technology – talk to text software. • A person to scribe. • Templates, highly scaffolded written tasks. • Reducing the volume of written work, choose quality over quantity. • Offer alternative assessment or practices, such as oral assessments and presentations. (ChildMind.org, 2024; Disability Standards for Education, 2024)

Lesson planning to accommodate impaired executive function

Take this student study of Isaiah. His key details were:

1. Assessed by an Educational Psychologist. He presents with an intellectual domain strength in science, IQ of 135, and a learning deficit, ADHD.
2. He is a friendly, chatty, and sensitive year 3 student in a mixed ability class of 28 same aged peers, 3 of whom are gifted.

3. Displays high anxiety, short working memory and slow processing, yet exhibits confidence when discussing his interests and strengths which are science and visual arts.
4. Affective support; regular counselling for anxiety and self-regulation strategies.
5. Academic support; Individual Education Plan with goals for science and visual arts.

Sample lesson

Differentiated and scaffolded for impaired executive function

Experiment	Learning Outcomes: Yr. 3 (VCSSU058), Yr. 4 (VCSIS050).
Know	• The repetitive nature of lifecycles. • Patterns and relationships are present throughout the lifecycle process.
Understand	• Plants and fungus respond to their environment and change. • Plants and fungus are created differently.
Do	• Dissect and describe the internal features of a tulip head or fungi cap. • Predict, examine, and record observations.
Tier 2 *Core lesson	• Choose a tulip from the selection as your specimen. Label the components of the flower/stem. Record as a drawing or photo. • Make a prediction about what you think each portion contains. • Dissect with scissors and make a cross section. • Use the magnifying lamp to examine. • Record your observations on the observation sheet. • In what way was your prediction correct/incorrect? • Explain your findings as outline on the whiteboard in your Lifecycle journal.

Tier 3 *Differentiated lesson (High ability group move to withdraw room)	• Choose a tulip and a fungus specimen. Label the components of the flower and mushroom. Record as a drawing or photo. • Make a prediction about what you think the flower head and mushroom cap/gills contain. • Dissect using the slicing tool and tweezers the flower head and mushroom cap/gills. • Use the probe to pull apart. • Analyse with the microscope. • Distinguish how the specimens' cross-sections vary. • In what way was your prediction correct/incorrect? • Explain your findings on the observation organiser or the Dictaphone with talk-to-text.

(VCAA CURRICULUM RESOURCES AND SUPPORT, 2024).

Explaining scaffolding for impaired functions

Through the application of Brown's model (2005), impaired functions are appropriately scaffolded.

Aid activation

- Activation can be initiated with visual planners, digital technology, and verbal teacher re-enforcement 1:1.
- Reduce expectations – graphic organisers reduce the enormity of expectations and incorporate dot-point notations to capture ideas quickly.
- Documentation amendments – break tasks down or chunk for note taking, provide scaffolded samples.
- Repetition – although basic content and factual repetition have been eliminated, instructional repetition is required, write on the whiteboard.

Support effort and memory

- Effort and memory impairments impact the utilisation of thought processing and working memory. Therefore, regardless of age, concrete examples must be provided. These can be as simple as a worked example of an essay or a final product to view.

- Assistance technology is key – digital recording equipment, dictation software, photos, film, typed documents etc all support slow processing speeds, enhance organisation, and promote learning activation.

Sustain focus and regulate actions

- Environmental changes – a quiet room required with minimal distractions can reduce the volume of disengaged moments. Providing room for physical movement, allowing students to stand while working or take a brain-break help self-regulation.
- Higher order cognitive skills sustain engagement by interlinking broader science knowledge and enabling synthesis to create deeper meanings.
- The experiment plays to Ben's strengths and interests which further support focus and engagement as hands-on-learning guides him to deeper thinking and the transferral of his broader science understanding to explain his predictions, thoughts, and reasoning, practically apply his knowledge.

(Anderson et al., 2001; DET, 2023; Maker, 2009; Brown, 2013; NAGC, 2019).

Example of scaffolded assessment task

A variety of methods were used to assess Isaiah's capabilities. If he was required to sit a written test, with a time limit, he may have done poorly due to his executive function limitations.

Implemented via the class *Science Teams* folder.

- Interactive quizzes: for knowledge and understanding.
- Think-pair-share: for collaborative problem solving.
- Digital exit tickets: open ended questions and student feedback. Teacher to assess and respond.
- Comic strip summaries: key concepts or ideas are drawn and explained.
- 1:1 learning conversations: recorded for I.E.P and anecdotal notes.
- Observations: self-regulation observations to support I.C.P.

Executive function and communication challenges

Asha, a 2e ADHD student, regularly grappled with communication misinterpretation. Whether it was her inability to control her free-flow chatter, or, her over sensitive responses. Firstly, her loud chatter, laughter and impulsive interjections, impacted the group dynamics by frequently derailing their conversations. Although her friends found her entertaining and funny, there were times when they mistook Asha's verbal impulsivity and physical hyperactivity as being 'too over the top'. Additionally, with the presence of high distractibility, she struggled to remain engaged in detailed, lengthy conversations that required sustained listening, often zoning out and missing parts of the information being shared. Yet, Asha's sensitive and empathetic nature, meant her peers would confide in her seeking her compassion and relying on her strengths in advocacy. Internally, however, the simmering anxiety that always lay beneath the surface would often reduce her ability to clearly process and interpret pertinent details being shared, leaving portions of the information either misinterpreted or completely overlooked.

Conversely, the communication challenges Moses encountered due to ASD, were vastly different. His hurdles included the minimal eye contact he would give to others and his literal interpretation of words and phrases, which impacted him as he struggled to grasp the slang, banter, and jokes his peers were laughing at. Although he desired to engage with the group, he found it hard to keep pace with their non-verbal cues, sarcastic comments, as well as process the dialogue to generate an answer. Additionally, his traits of social anxiety and some repetitive behaviours, were viewed by his neurotypical peers as confronting and odd.

Although Asha and Moses experienced vastly different communication challenges, the emotional outcomes were similar. Despite their best efforts, they were left feeling misunderstood, worried about peer rejection, and loneliness and their naturally heightened anxiety, often made school days gruelling (Cross, 2023; Leonard, 2024).

Encouraging clear communication

As good communication is essential in most aspects of life, whether in personal or professional environments, successful communication requires two key skills:

1. *Intra*-personal skills are internal and support an individual to process their thoughts and emotions.
2. *Inter*-personal skills are the ability to accurately interpret signals that others send and form an accurate response.

Research attests to the fact that for communication skills to increase and be strengthened, individuals will require an intervention method that is tailored specially to their need so the best support can be delivered (Honeybourne, 2018). Common approaches include.

- Social skills therapy/coaching
    - awareness of how to interpret/display non-verbal cues.
    - manage impulsive interjections.
    - practice clear, concise, and specific expectations that can minimise confusion.
    - training the individual to receive critical feedback for growth, not a personal attack
- Medication
    - increases motivation and attention while reducing the severity of verbal impulsivity, interjections, and mental distraction.
- High importance discussions
    - schedule agreed times to discuss important issues.
    - providing the 'topic' ahead of time allows for greater intellectual, emotional and thought processing prior to the chat.

Managing communication and emotional responses

'Listening Plan': *In THE moment*

A simple communication platform between the student and teacher designed as an immediate conversation when the child is overwhelmed:

1. The teacher/student use cues to indicate the need for a private chat.
2. The student expresses the feelings or sensations they are experiencing – in that moment.
3. Teacher/student decide a solution appropriate for that setting and act on it there and then.
4. This is a proactive approach for self-regulation and positive behaviour choices before a 'melt down' occurs.

'Rescue Plan': *Pre-planned*
- An agreed plan with previously agreed rescue behaviours and tools.
- These are accessible so the student can manage a situation independently and respond in the critical moment the child is struggling.

'Rescue Tools': *Keep on hand*
- Items used to assist the agreed rescue plan, e.g. fidget toys, noise reducing headphones, wobble cushions, weighted packs, scribble books, question/ideas book, ice pack, cold water, chewing items or mints etc.

(Australian Online Courses, 2024; Cross, 2024; Honeybourne, 2018; DiTullio, 2018)

Improving executive function strategies

Modifications
- Content, process, product, testing and assessments.
- Scaffolded tasks, talk-to-text, scribe, immersive reading software, task exemplars, organisation prompts, timers, iPads and laptops.

Oral instruction
- Reinforce 2 key instructions at a time – student retells then actions.
- Repeat in chunks of 2.

Visual instruction
- Dot point instructions on board/paper in sets of 2.
- Large spacing between each set of 2

Chunking information
- Present information in small, manageable chunks.
- Break down complex tasks into sequential steps.
- Provide clear guidance on how to complete each step.

Create independence
- Provide a work sample of the expected product.
- Offer steps to trouble shooting – before – seeking help.
- Colour-code workbooks so they are easy to identify in a bag or locker. Large class timetable and routines on the board and desk.

Short, frequent tasks
- Break down lessons into smaller, manageable tasks. Provide opportunities for brief breaks or movement between tasks.

Direct content
- Give clear, concise content. Repeat key information, summarise in 2 or 3 points to ensure key content has registered.

Visual planning
- Map out large projects. Break tasks into manageable pieces and plot on a calendar to show when each portion is due.

Recapping
- Recap previous key points from the last lesson of the subject before new learning.
- Quick oral retelling helps the student to 'tune in'.

Positive reinforcement
- Implement a reward system that emphasises positive organisation improvements.
- Provide immediate feedback and encouragement for progress.

(Cross, 2024; DiTullio, 2018)

Presentation of written material
- Scaffolded work sheets.
- Teacher reduces the volume of text to dot points.
- Clear, typed script – Comic Sans or Arial font.
- Font size 12–14, dark text on a light background.
- 20% larger headings and extra spaces around paragraphing.
- Bold text, no underlining.
- Reduce pictorial distractions to a minimum.
- Explain non-literal language.
- Clear, simple sentences for instructions.
- Exclude pink, red, green coloured paper or text colour.
- Small volumes of written text that is concise.
- Write in an active voice, highlight key words.
- Instructions should be direct.

Supporting Concentration and Sensory Responses

Environment

- Natural or soft lighting, quiet withdrawal spaces, and a soothing interior colour scheme.
- Low noise, with an area that has reduced audio/visual stimulus.
- Use of pictorial cues, timetables and clear work surfaces.
- De-clutter rooms and spaces.
- Equipment such as earmuffs/headphones/earplugs, sunglasses or tinted reading glasses, weighted packs, fidget toys, natural/soft lighting.
- Flexible seating, standing desks or bench, quiet corner or withdrawal room.

Physical

- Movement breaks.
- *'Tapping'* pressure points.
- Brain break.
- Deep breathing.

(Cross, 2024; DiTullio, 2018)

# KEY TAKEAWAYS

- **Teachers' role in supporting 2e students:** Teachers play a critical role in shaping the lives of twice-exceptional (2e) students by combining knowledge of cognitive, social, and neurological development with curriculum expertise. However, many feel underprepared to meet the diverse needs of these students, particularly due to misunderstandings about neurological impairments and their permanence.

- **Understanding executive function:** Executive functions encompass cognitive processes like planning, working memory, and self-regulation. These interconnected mental processes are often impaired in 2e students, affecting their ability to focus, organise, and sustain effort. Brown's (2005) model provides a clear framework for understanding these impairments and how they manifest in educational settings.

- **Tailored teaching practices for specific needs:** Effective teaching for 2e students requires tailored practices such as reducing distractions, breaking tasks into manageable chunks, and using assistive technologies. Specific strategies vary depending on conditions like ADHD, ASD, dyslexia, or dysgraphia, but all emphasise scaffolding and individualised support.

- **Scaffolding and modifications:** Scaffolding strategies, such as using visual planners, task chunking, and assistive technologies, help mitigate executive function impairments. These approaches enable 2e students to better manage tasks, sustain focus, and engage with curriculum content at their level of ability.

- **Communication and emotional regulation:** Supporting communication and emotional regulation is vital for 2e students, who often struggle with impulsivity, misunderstandings, or emotional overwhelm. Strategies like social skills therapy, tailored rescue plans, and clear, concise instructions help build confidence and resilience in both academic and social settings.

Chapter references

ADHD Foundation. (2021). Supporting students with ADHD in educational settings. Retrieved from https://adhdfoundation.org.uk

Anderson, L. W., Krathwohl, D. R., Airasian, P. W., Cruikshank, K. A., Mayer, R. E., Pintrich, P. R., Raths, J., & Wittrock, M. C. (2001). *A taxonomy for learning, teaching, and assessing: A revision of Bloom's taxonomy of educational objectives.* Longman.

Atkins, S. (2020). Understanding twice-exceptional learners: Connecting research to practice. *Teaching Exceptional Children, 52*(4), 216–228.

Australian Online Courses. (2024). Strategies for supporting students with specific learning difficulties. Retrieved from https://www.australianonlinecourses.com.au

Baumer, J. (2021). Dyslexia and executive function: Addressing the overlap. *Journal of Learning Disabilities, 54*(3), 238–248. https://doi.org/10.1177/0022219420972156

Brown Clinic for Attention & Related Disorders. (2024). Understanding executive functions. Retrieved from https://www.brownadhdclinic.com/resources

Brown, T. E. (2005). *Attention deficit disorder: The unfocused mind in children and adults.* Yale University Press.

ChildMind.org. (2024). Understanding dysgraphia in children. Retrieved from https://childmind.org/guide/dysgraphia/

Cross, C. (2024). Executive function strategies for twice-exceptional learners: A practical guide for educators. *Teaching Exceptional Children, 56*(3), 145–157.

Cross, T. L. (2023). Supporting the emotional needs of twice-exceptional learners. *Gifted Child Today, 46*(1), 36–44. https://doi.org/10.1177/1076217522113298

Department of Education and Training [DET]. (2023). Supporting students with diverse learning needs. Victorian Government. Retrieved from https://www.education.vic.gov.au

Disability Standards for Education. (2024). Australian Government Department of Education. Retrieved from https://www.education.gov.au

DiTullio, C. (2018). Strategies for helping students with ADHD succeed in school. *Educational Leadership, 76*(1), 50–55.

Goldstein, S., Naglieri, J. A., Princiotta, D., & Otero, T. M. (Eds.). (2014). *Handbook of executive functioning.* Springer.

Honeybourne, V. (2018). *The neurodiverse classroom: A teacher's guide to individual learning needs and how to meet them.* Jessica Kingsley Publishers.

Leonard, H. (2024). Supporting twice-exceptional students in inclusive classrooms. *Australian Journal of Special Education, 48*(2), 75–92. https://doi.org/10.1017/ajse.2024.6

Lucas, R., & Soares, L. (2013). Neuroscience and learning: Implications for teaching practice. *Journal of Neuroscience and Education, 5*(2), 85–96.

Maker, C. J. (2009). Curriculum differentiation for gifted students. In B. MacFarlane & T. Stambaugh (Eds.), *Leading change in gifted education* (pp. 227–248). Prufrock Press.

National Association for Gifted Children [NAGC]. (2019). Position statement: Twice-exceptional learners. Retrieved from https://www.nagc.org/position-statements

National Association for Gifted and Talented Children. (2021). Twice-exceptional learners: Challenges and strategies. Retrieved from https://www.nagc.org

Peterson, J. S. (2016). Addressing the needs of gifted students with disabilities. *Psychology in the Schools, 53*(10), 1146–1156. https://doi.org/10.1002/pits.21965

Posner, M. I. (1975). Psychobiology of attention. In M. S. Gazzaniga & C. Blakemore (Eds.), *Handbook of psychobiology* (pp. 441–480). Academic Press.

VCAA Curriculum Resources and Support. (2024). Victorian curriculum F–10: Science. Victorian Curriculum and Assessment Authority. Retrieved from https://victoriancurriculum.vcaa.vic.edu.au/science/

The President and Fellows of Harvard College. (2024). Executive function and self-regulation: Skills for life and learning. Retrieved from https://developingchild.harvard.edu

CHAPTER 6
Emotions R Us: Triumph Tempered by Fear and Failure

Nina Thomas

The emotional landscape

In the vibrant landscape of education, emotions are the colourful threads that run through every student's learning journey. For twice-exceptional students, these emotional experiences can be especially complex, with high peaks of excitement and deep valleys of frustration. This chapter focuses on how educators can help 2e students navigate these emotional ups and downs, fostering a supportive environment that allows them to embrace, understand, and manage their feelings.

At the core of the 2e student's emotional experience is a unique contrast – the elation of success often juxtaposed with intense moments of frustration or self-doubt. Imagine a student who excels in grasping complex mathematical concepts, feeling the thrill of mastering advanced problems. Yet, in the next moment, they might struggle with a writing task, exposing challenges like dysgraphia. These students can shift from the euphoria of academic achievement to the despair of feeling inadequate within the same day, the same lesson even the same activity. They may shine brightly in one area but feel crushed by challenges in another, creating an emotional rollercoaster that can be hard for both the student and their teachers to navigate.

During moments of success, these students may feel invincible, basking in the recognition and praise that accompany their achievements. But with every challenge or stumble – especially in areas where their learning differences are most apparent – their confidence can quickly erode. The emotional impact of academic struggles for 2e students can be particularly profound. They may begin to question their abilities, even doubting their place in an academic setting. This cycle of elation and despondency can lead to self-criticism, isolation, and a fragile sense of self-worth.

As educators, understanding the emotional spectrum of 2e students is crucial. By acknowledging the intensity of their highs and lows and providing them with strategies to manage these emotions, we can help them build resilience. Offering praise for effort, normalising mistakes as part of learning, and creating an inclusive, empathetic classroom environment can empower 2e students to not only recognise their strengths but also navigate their challenges with greater confidence and emotional stability.

For twice-exceptional students, success can be a double-edged sword. While academic achievements may initially boost their confidence and validate their talents, there is often a lingering fear of not being able to maintain those high standards. The pressure to consistently perform – whether from themselves or societal expectations – can be overwhelming, leading to heightened anxiety and self-doubt. Their self-confidence becomes intricately tied to their academic journey, with each success overshadowed by the fear of future failure, and every setback magnified by the weight of their insecurities. This fragile emotional balance is shaped not only by academic struggles but also by the interplay of internal expectations and external pressures. Navigating this emotional landscape requires resilience, support, and an understanding of their unique strengths and vulnerabilities, highlighting the need for a teaching approach that transcends the binary of success and failure.

The concept of "flow," introduced by renowned psychologist Mihaly Csikszentmihalyi (2014), offers valuable insight into the emotional experiences of 2e students. Csikszentmihalyi's research in positive psychology focuses on achieving optimal experiences and what makes life worth living. "Flow" describes a state of complete immersion and engagement in an activity, where individuals lose track of time and experience deep enjoyment and intrinsic motivation. This state is achieved when there is a balance between the challenge of the task and the individual's skill level, leading to a sense of effortless involvement and peak performance.

Consider a creatively gifted student who excels in endeavours such as art or music but struggles with organisation and time management. For these students, moments of artistic expression evoke a profound sense of flow, where they feel fully engaged and energised by their creative process. However, outside the realm of their artistic pursuits, they encounter obstacles that disrupt their flow and trigger feelings of frustration and self-doubt. The practical demands of academic life, such as deadlines and assignments, feel stifling and overwhelming to individuals who thrive on spontaneity and creative exploration. As a result, they struggle to navigate the structured environment of traditional education, feeling constrained by the rigidity of academic expectations.

This dichotomy of emotions creates a constant tension between their passion for their craft and the practical demands of academic life. On one hand, they experience moments of elation and fulfilment when expressing themselves through their chosen medium, revelling in the freedom and creativity it affords them. On the other hand, they grapple with feelings of inadequacy and self-doubt when confronted with tasks that require linear thinking and adherence to deadlines.

Moreover, the pressure to excel academically intensifies their emotional struggles, as they feel compelled to prioritise academic performance over their creative pursuits. This internal conflict undermines their confidence and sense of identity as they struggle to reconcile their passion for creativity with societal expectations of success.

Understanding emotional complexity

2e students often experience heightened sensitivities, feeling emotions with greater depth and complexity than their neurotypical peers (Killgore et al., 2017). This emotional intensity can be both a burden and a gift, magnifying the impact of failures while amplifying the satisfaction of successes. Their emotional experiences are vivid and intense, manifesting in various ways, including strong reactions to success or failure, a profound sense of justice, and deep empathy for others. For example, a 2e student might experience extreme highs after an academic success but plummet into deep frustration after a minor setback. This emotional spectrum makes them uniquely attuned to their environment but also vulnerable to emotional overload.

A notable aspect of their sensitivity is their reaction to sensory stimuli. For example, bright lights, loud noises, or strong smells that may go unnoticed by peers can overwhelm a 2e student, triggering emotional responses ranging from discomfort to distress (De Bonte & Silverman, 2024). This can affect their ability to focus and engage in the classroom. Additionally, disruptions to routine, such as a sudden schedule change or unexpected events, can evoke intense emotional reactions, as 2e students often rely on predictability for a sense of security (De Bonte et al., 2024). Physical symptoms like headaches or stomach aches may accompany their emotional responses. Furthermore, 2e students often demonstrate heightened empathy, deeply connecting with the emotions of others (Lovecky, 2023). While this can foster strong relationships and a deep sense of compassion, it can also become overwhelming, as they may absorb the emotions of those around them, leading to emotional exhaustion. Their heightened sensitivity shapes their daily interactions and experiences, influencing how they perceive and navigate the world.

Creating an emotionally inclusive environment

An emotionally inclusive classroom is a space where all students, especially twice-exceptional learners, feel safe, understood, and valued. It prioritises emotional wellbeing by fostering open dialogue and encouraging empathy and acceptance. In this environment, 2e students are encouraged to express their emotions openly and engage in meaningful conversations about their unique experiences. Teachers play a crucial role, using tools like emotional wheels (see Figure 1 and Figure 2) to help students articulate their feelings, while group work is structured to accommodate diverse communication styles, ensuring all students feel heard and included. Mindfulness practices are integrated to promote self-regulation and emotional resilience, creating a foundation for students to manage their emotions effectively. Additionally, sensory-friendly accommodations, such as quieter spaces or dimmed lighting, help students with heightened sensitivities focus and participate without feeling overwhelmed.

There are two ways to use the emotion wheel: as a two-dimensional circle or as a three-dimensional ellipse. When used as a two-dimensional circle (see Figure 1) the individual can dive into the wheel to explore their primary emotions – such as joy, anger, or fear – and see how these primary emotions combine to create secondary emotions like awe, remorse, aggression, and optimism (Roeckelein, 2006). This allows for deeper self-reflection and helps individuals identify not only what they're feeling but also the complexity and nuances of those emotions.

Figure 1: The Two-Dimensional Emotion Wheel

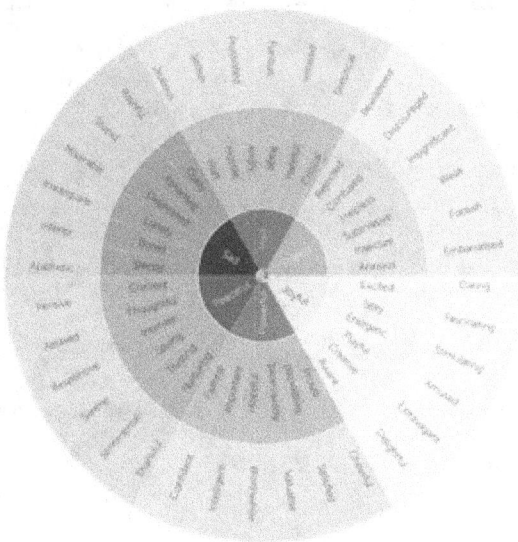

In its three-dimensional form Figure 2, the wheel highlights the emotional intensity of both primary and secondary emotions, helping individuals gauge not just what they are feeling but how strongly they are experiencing those emotions (Roeckelein, 2006).

Figure 2: The Three-Dimensional Emotion Wheel.

- **Survival Issues**

  „Organisms at all evolutionary levels face certain common functional survival problems."

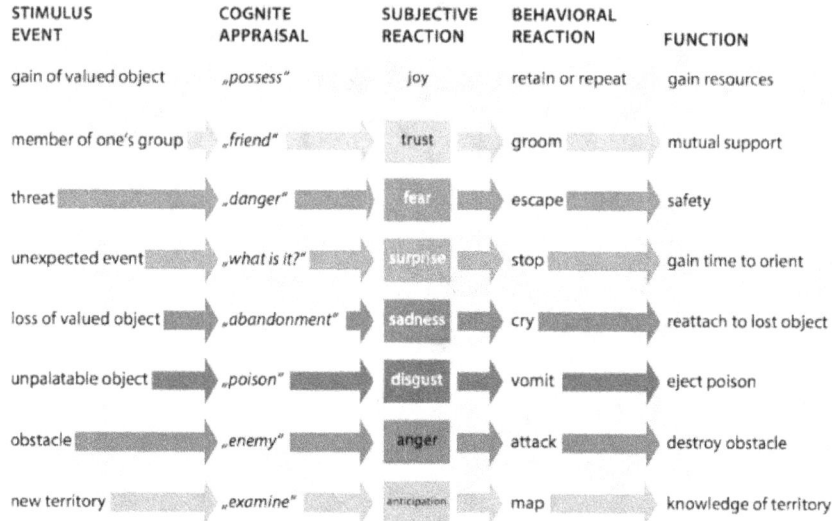

According to Plutchik's Sequential Model (1961; 2001; 2007), emotions are activated in response to specific stimuli and lead to certain behavioural patterns necessary for survival (Krohn, 2007). Plutchik identified several core behaviours tied to emotional responses:

- **Protection** (activated by fear) results in behaviours like withdrawal or retreat.
- **Destruction** (activated by anger) drives efforts to eliminate barriers.
- **Incorporation** (activated by acceptance) relates to consuming or receiving nourishment.
- **Rejection** (activated by disgust) prompts the removal of harmful materials.
- **Reproduction** (activated by joy) encourages bonding and pleasure.
- **Reintegration** (activated by sadness) is the response to loss.
- **Exploration** (activated by curiosity) motivates investigation and play.

- **Orientation** (activated by surprise) occurs in reaction to new or unfamiliar stimuli (Screenr, 2017).

These emotional responses happen largely on a subconscious level, with each emotion prompting a specific survival behaviour. Understanding this framework allows individuals to recognise that emotions are not just fleeting feelings but are deeply connected to behaviours that have evolved to help us navigate and respond to our environments.

Below is a table from the International Handbook of Emotions in Education. It shows the relationship between these various factors and sub-systems, as well as their presumed functions (Pekrun & Linnenbrink-Garica, 2014)

Table of Emotional Relationship Between these Various Factors and Sub-Systems

Component	Primary Function	Examples
Subjective feeling	Monitoring	Sadness, happiness, gratitude, anger, feeling good
Action tendency	Motivation	Urge to weep, to jump up and down, to approach
Appraisal	Meaning making	I just lost something; I just received a gift; I passed a difficult test, something good happened to me
Motor activity	Communication	Crying, smiling, raising one's chin, making oneself small, moving one's arms up and down quickly
Physiological	Support	Changes in pulse, blood flow, brain activity

(PEKRUN & LINNENBRINK-GARICA, 2014)

Open dialogue and communication

Open dialogue is a cornerstone in creating an emotionally inclusive classroom, fostering trust, mutual respect, and encouraging a culture of open communication (Maxwell & Gurin, 2017). Picture a classroom where the teacher holds weekly meetings dedicated to discussing emotions and personal experiences, allowing students to express their thoughts in a safe, non-judgemental space where their voices are valued. For instance, in one session, the focus might be on resilience. The teacher introduces the concept, explaining how resilience helps us overcome challenges, and invites students to reflect on times when they demonstrated resilience in their own lives. As students share stories – whether it's pushing through a tough soccer match or excelling in a difficult math test – some may express frustration or anxiety, while others share coping strategies they've developed.

This open dialogue gives students insight into their own emotions and builds empathy for their peers. They learn to listen actively, offer support, and celebrate each other's successes (Maxwell & Gurin, 2017). The teacher reinforces the idea that everyone faces challenges differently, but together they can overcome them. To further encourage emotional expression, the teacher might incorporate journal prompts into daily activities, asking questions like, "Describe a time you felt proud of yourself," or "What is a challenge you're currently facing, and how are you coping?" These prompts offer students a private, reflective space to process their emotions (Karimova, 2017).

However, as students' progress into secondary and senior secondary education, maintaining this kind of open dialogue becomes more challenging. Teachers may not always encounter students in emotional moments, and the transient nature of class schedules can limit these opportunities (Maxwell & Gurin, 2017). Additionally, specific learning disabilities, particularly those related to writing, present another layer of complexity (Gardner, 2007). In these cases, accommodations like voice-to-text technology or integrating ICT can ensure fairness. A clip-on microphone, for example, allows students to share their thoughts privately without being overpowering, preserving both dignity and privacy (Lee, 2011; MacArthur & Cavalier, 2004). By adapting these methods, teachers can continue fostering a culture of openness, ensuring all students – regardless of their learning needs – feel supported in expressing their emotions and building resilience.

Group work

In the bustling classroom, envision a group project where students are brainstorming ideas and delegating tasks. As discussions unfold, subtle social dynamics emerge: some students naturally take charge, confidently voicing their opinions, while others prefer to contribute more quietly. The room hums with activity, but emotions can rise as debates become heated. Here, the educator's role becomes essential. By guiding structured discussions and introducing communication techniques such as active listening, assertive expression, and constructive feedback, the teacher creates an environment where students can thrive collaboratively (Peterson et al., 2019; Srikanth et al., 2016). For example, during a reflection session, the educator may ask students to consider how various communication styles influenced their group's outcomes. This exercise helps students not only to reflect on their interactions but also to recognise how their own communication approaches impacted group dynamics (Gurung & Landrum, 2014).

Through this process, students receive constructive peer feedback, which is instrumental in helping them understand their communication preferences and how they influence group collaboration. Skills like active listening and respecting diverse perspectives become integral parts of their learning (Srikanth et al., 2016). They begin to see the value of adapting their communication style to foster better teamwork, learning how to engage in collaborative decision-making, support one another, and remain flexible in their problem-solving approaches.

By navigating these social dynamics, students not only enhance their academic performance but also develop vital interpersonal skills. Conflict resolution strategies, such as reframing disagreements into constructive discussions, are key to maintaining positive group interactions (Peterson et al., 2019). These experiences prepare students for future professional and personal interactions, where understanding and managing different communication styles are essential for success. As a result, students leave with a deeper appreciation for diversity, collaboration, and the power of working together toward common goals (Gurung & Landrum, 2014).

Mindfulness

Mindfulness practices are essential in supporting the emotional wellbeing of 2e students by offering effective tools to help them manage their emotions. Techniques such as deep breathing, guided imagery, and mindful awareness of emotions foster self-regulation, allowing students to feel calm and centered amid the complexities of their academic and social lives (Sisk, 2021; Zenner et al., 2014). Beyond traditional relaxation techniques, mindfulness can also include sensory-engaging activities like colouring, sketching, or working with clay.

These activities encourage focused attention, immersing students in the present moment and help them cultivate a deeper sense of mindfulness (Zenner et al., 2014). Research shows that mindfulness can increase grey matter density in brain regions associated with memory, learning, and emotional regulation, such as the hippocampus and prefrontal cortex, leading to improved cognitive function and emotional resilience over time (Fox et al., 2014; Hölzel et al., 2011; Tang et al., 2015). For 2e students, whose minds often race with rapid thoughts, mindfulness slows down mental activity, reducing stress and enhancing both concentration and emotional balance (Tang et al., 2015).

Educators play a crucial role in modelling mindfulness practices, promoting self-care and emotional awareness to create a culture of wellbeing in the classroom (Sisk, 2021). For example, a teacher who notices that students often feel overwhelmed by academic pressures or social challenges might introduce a daily mindfulness routine to help alleviate stress. Each morning, the teacher could guide the class through a few minutes of deep breathing exercises, explaining how this practice can manage stress and improve focus. Simple phrases like, "Let's take a few deep breaths to start the day feeling calm and ready to learn," help reinforce the value of mindfulness. To further create a peaceful environment, the teacher might incorporate quiet activities such as colouring or listening to soft music, helping students ease into the day.

Over time, students begin to look forward to these routines, recognising how mindfulness makes them feel more relaxed, focused, and better equipped to manage academic challenges (Zenner et al., 2014). Importantly, because mindfulness is practiced as a whole-class activity, it doesn't single out students with additional needs. Instead, it serves as an inclusive strategy that benefits everyone, including the teacher, fostering a calm and supportive learning environment that enhances emotional wellbeing and engagement for all (Fox et al., 2014; Tang et al., 2015).

Sensory challenges

Heightened sensitivity is a hallmark of twice-exceptional (2e) students, highlighting the complexity of their emotional and sensory experiences. Everyday environments can become overwhelming for these students, as sensory stimuli such as lights, sounds, and smells provoke strong emotional reactions (Gere et al., 2009; Wu et al., 2019; Jarrard, 2023). Recognising and accommodating these sensitivities is crucial in supporting their learning and overall wellbeing.

Figure 3: Signs of Sensory Overload

HTTPS://IMAGES.SQUARESPACE-CDN.COM/CONTENT/V1/60D2550DE332B22F60EEC9F4/2AEEAEAA-0C68-4DC8-8782-2DBCF31AB699/SENSORY+OVERLOAD.PNG?FORMAT=500W

Case example: David

David is a 2e student who excels in history but is highly sensitive to sensory inputs that others might tolerate easily. During class presentations, David becomes overwhelmed by the combination of bright lights, the rustling of papers, whispers, and the smell of markers. These sensory triggers cause him to feel anxious, distracted, and unable to focus on the task. To help David succeed, his teacher needs to implement accommodations tailored to his sensory needs.

Strategy	Description	Application in David's Case
Create a sensory-friendly environment	Design the classroom to reduce sensory overload by using soft lighting, noise-cancelling headphones, and air purifiers.	Provide David with noise-cancelling headphones during presentations and reduce the brightness of lights or use desk lamps.
Offer flexible seating options	Provide a variety of seating options like bean bags, wobble chairs, or stability balls to enhance comfort.	Allow David to sit in a more comfortable seat, like a bean bag or stability ball, to reduce discomfort and aid focus.
Use visual supports	Utilise visual schedules, emotion charts, and social stories to provide structure and reduce anxiety.	Provide David with a visual schedule outlining the day's tasks, helping him anticipate transitions and reduce anxiety.
Provide sensory breaks	Allow students to take short breaks to decompress, such as stretching or using fidget tools.	Offer David sensory breaks when overwhelmed, such as stepping outside for fresh air or using a stress ball during lessons.
Offer alternative assignments	Adapt assignments to avoid overwhelming sensory input, such as providing written instructions or quiet settings.	Allow David to complete tasks in a quieter setting or provide written instructions for assignments instead of verbal ones.

Strategy	Description	Application in David's Case
Implement sensory diet strategies	Collaborate with specialists to develop a personalised sensory diet plan to regulate sensory input.	Work with David's occupational therapist to incorporate specific sensory activities, like deep breathing exercises, into his day.
Educate peers and staff	Raise awareness about sensory sensitivities and encourage empathy and understanding among students and staff.	Educate David's peers about sensory processing differences and train staff on how to recognise signs of sensory overload.

Case example: Emma

Emma is a twice-exceptional (2e) student who demonstrates exceptional writing abilities but struggles with organisation and focus due to her ADHD. While her creative writing skills allow her to construct intricate narratives, she finds it difficult to structure her thoughts when working within rigid academic constraints. This often results in frustration and self-doubt, particularly when assignments require detailed planning, strict deadlines, or extensive revisions.

Emma's struggles extend beyond academic tasks. She frequently experiences difficulties in maintaining focus during long class periods, and her rapid thoughts often lead to forgetfulness or difficulty following multi-step instructions. Despite her intellectual strengths, these executive functioning challenges contribute to feelings of inadequacy and anxiety, particularly when she perceives that she is falling behind her peers.

Focus Area	Strategy	Application in Emma's Case
Resilience	Develop emotional regulation, problem-solving skills, and a growth mindset.	Emma struggles with staying organised due to her ADHD. Educators can help her see challenges as learning opportunities, building her resilience.

Focus Area	Strategy	Application in Emma's Case
Mindfulness practices	Incorporate mindfulness techniques (e.g., deep breathing, self-awareness) to aid self-regulation.	Emma learns to recognise moments of distraction and uses mindfulness techniques to redirect her focus without judgement.
Growth mindset	Reinforce the belief that skills and abilities improve with effort and practice.	Teachers encourage Emma to view her organisational struggles as areas for improvement rather than fixed limitations, fostering a growth mindset.
Cognitive Behavioural Techniques (CBT)	Integrate mindfulness techniques like CBT to alter negative thought patterns.	Emma observes her thoughts during moments of disorganisation and gently reorients her focus, improving self-regulation over time.
Self-advocacy	Teach self-awareness and communication of needs.	Through reflective journaling, Emma recognises how ADHD affects her writing and identifies when she needs help with assignments.
Role-playing for communication	Use role-playing exercises to practice asking for accommodations and support.	Emma practices asking her teachers for extra time on assignments or a quieter workspace when she feels overwhelmed.
Promoting independence	Provide choices and autonomy in learning tasks to build confidence and agency.	Emma is allowed to choose her own writing topics and task order, fostering a sense of ownership over her learning process.

Focus Area	Strategy	Application in Emma's Case
Support network	Build a strong support network, including peers, mentors, and family.	Emma's teacher encourages her to join a writing club, where she connects with peers who appreciate her creative talents, boosting her confidence.
Mentorship opportunities	Connect Emma with older peers or adults who have faced similar challenges for guidance.	Emma is paired with a mentor who has successfully navigated ADHD, offering practical advice and emotional support.

By using strategies such as mindfulness, self-advocacy, and a growth mindset, Emma can better manage the challenges of ADHD while strengthening her resilience and independence. These tools help her not only navigate academic pressures but also build the emotional and social skills necessary to thrive in both educational and personal contexts.

Building resilience and self-advocacy is particularly important for 2e students as it gives them the skills to equip them to handle the unique challenges they face. Resilience helps them persevere through difficulties, while self-advocacy ensures they receive the necessary support and accommodations. Together, these skills foster a sense of empowerment, enabling 2e students to navigate their educational journeys more effectively and confidently.

Navigating academic challenges

Twice-exceptional (2e) students often experience a complex mix of academic strengths and challenges, and resilience is key to helping them persevere through difficulties. By viewing setbacks as opportunities for growth rather than failures, these students can maintain motivation and engagement in their education (Duyar, Özkaya & Akdeniz, 2023). For example, in the previous case study, Emma's advanced writing abilities are sometimes overshadowed by her ADHD, which causes her to lose focus or struggle with organisation. Resilience enables her to view these challenges as part of her learning journey, not insurmountable obstacles. By developing a growth mindset, she learns to appreciate her progress and remains determined to improve (Dweck, 2013).

Here are a series of ideas to help navigate these challenges:

Enhancing social skills and relationships

Social interactions can be particularly challenging for 2e students, who may feel isolated due to their unique combination of abilities and difficulties. Building resilience helps them navigate social setbacks, such as misunderstandings or conflicts with peers, and continue to seek out meaningful connections. This is essential for their emotional wellbeing and social development (Duyar, Özkaya & Akdeniz, 2023).

Self-advocacy plays a crucial role in helping 2e students communicate their needs and strengths to others. By effectively expressing themselves, they can foster understanding and support from peers and teachers, reducing feelings of isolation and promoting inclusivity. For Emma, learning to articulate her experiences with ADHD can help her classmates better understand her behaviour, leading to a more supportive social environment (Reis, Baum & Burke, 2014).

Promoting independence and empowerment

Resilience and self-advocacy empower 2e students to take control of their learning and personal growth. As they become more self-aware and confident in their abilities to overcome challenges, they develop a greater sense of autonomy. This independence is vital for their long-term success, both in and out of the classroom (Reis, Baum & Burke, 2014).

Encouraging 2e students to advocate for themselves teaches them valuable life skills, such as problem-solving, negotiation, and self-regulation. These skills are not only important for academic achievement, but also for navigating future personal and professional environments. Emma, for example, will benefit from learning how to request the accommodations she needs, whether it's extra time on exams or a quieter workspace, setting her up for success in higher education and beyond (Carroll, 2023).

Building a supportive community

A key aspect of resilience and self-advocacy is the ability to build and rely on a supportive network. This network can include teachers, peers, family members, and mentors who understand and appreciate the unique challenges and strengths of 2e students. Fostering these connections allows students like Emma to draw on a wealth of resources and support systems that help them navigate their educational journey (Duyar, Özkaya & Akdeniz, 2023).

Educators play a pivotal role in this process by creating inclusive and supportive classroom environments. By understanding the importance of resilience and self-advocacy, they can implement strategies that not only address academic and social challenges but also celebrate the diverse talents of 2e students (Reis, Baum & Burke, 2014).

Creating an inclusive environment

Fostering an environment where diversity is not only acknowledged but actively celebrated is key to building an inclusive classroom, especially for twice-exceptional students. Educators should promote open dialogue about differences, encouraging mutual respect and understanding among students. One effective method is incorporating activities that highlight each student's unique strengths and talents, creating a culture that values individuality. These activities help bridge social gaps, encouraging students to view each other's uniqueness as valuable assets, enriching the overall learning experience (Duyar, Özkaya & Akdeniz, 2023).

Facilitating peer connections

Structured and informal opportunities for peer interaction play a critical role in fostering relationships, especially for 2e students who may struggle with social skills. Educators can implement group projects, collaborative activities, and peer mentoring programs designed to encourage teamwork and mutual support. Forming groups that leverage the strengths of 2e students while exposing them to diverse perspectives can enable them to excel academically and socially (Reis, Baum & Burke, 2014). Peer mentoring programs, where older students mentor 2e students, offer additional social support and positive role modelling. These structured interactions help create a classroom culture that not only values diversity but also supports the social development of all students, ensuring that 2e students feel connected and included (Duyar, Özkaya & Akdeniz, 2023).

Promoting social skills development

Explicitly teaching social skills through methods such as role-playing, group discussions, and social stories is particularly beneficial for 2e students. These approaches focus on developing key competencies like communication, empathy, problem-solving, and conflict resolution. Integrating Social-Emotional Learning (SEL) into the curriculum provides a structured framework for teaching these skills, emphasising self-awareness, social awareness, and relationship-building (Carroll, 2023).

Evidence-based SEL programs offer educators practical tools for helping students refine their social abilities (Carroll, 2023). By using literature, films, and real-life scenarios, educators can create engaging contexts for students to practice and enhance their social skills, ultimately fostering a sense of belonging and camaraderie among all students.

KEY TAKEAWAYS

- **The emotional rollercoaster of 2e students:** Twice-exceptional students experience a unique emotional spectrum, swinging between the elation of success and the frustration of challenges. This emotional intensity stems from their simultaneous strengths and weaknesses, which can lead to heightened self-doubt and fragile confidence, making emotional support critical.

- **The role of "flow" in emotional wellbeing:** Csikszentmihalyi's concept of "flow" highlights how 2e students thrive when their skills and challenges are balanced. For example, creative pursuits may immerse them in flow, whereas academic demands often disrupt this balance, causing frustration. Understanding flow can help educators create environments that foster engagement and satisfaction.

- **Heightened sensitivity in 2e students:** 2e students often display heightened emotional and sensory sensitivities. They may feel emotions more deeply than their peers and struggle with environmental stimuli, such as bright lights or loud noises. These sensitivities impact their focus, emotional regulation, and overall classroom experience, requiring tailored accommodations.

- **Building emotional resilience and self-advocacy:** Resilience and self-advocacy are essential skills for 2e students to navigate their emotional and academic challenges. Teaching students how to view setbacks as learning opportunities and articulate their needs builds their confidence and independence, preparing them for long-term success.

- **Creating an emotionally inclusive environment:** Teachers can foster emotional wellbeing in 2e students by creating an inclusive classroom environment. Techniques include open dialogue about emotions, mindfulness practices, structured group work to accommodate diverse needs, and sensory-friendly accommodations. These strategies help students feel safe, valued, and empowered to thrive academically and emotionally.

Chapter references

Carroll, L. S. (2023). Effective interventions to improve domain-specific social, emotional, or academic outcomes for twice-exceptional individuals who are gifted with ADHD as a disability. *Psychosomatic Medicine Research, 5*(4), 17. https://doi.org/10.53388/PSMR2023017

Csikszentmihalyi, M. (2014). *Flow: The psychology of optimal experience.* Harper Perennial Modern Classics.

De Bonte, C., & Silverman, L. K. (2024). Supporting 2e students with heightened sensitivities. *Journal of Gifted Education, 48*(1), 45-62.

Duyar, S. N., Özkaya, C., & Akdeniz, H. (2023). A systematic review of the factors affecting twice-exceptional students' social and emotional development. *Journal for the Education of the Gifted, 46*(3), 215-238. https://doi.org/10.1080/15332276.2023.2245861

Dweck, C. S. (2013). *Self-theories: Their role in motivation, personality, and development.* Taylor and Francis.

Fox, K. C. R., Nijeboer, S., Dixon, M. L., Floman, J. L., Ellamil, M., Rumak, S. P., Sedlmeier, P., & Christoff, K. (2014). Is meditation associated with altered brain structure? A systematic review and meta-analysis of morphometric neuroimaging in meditation practitioners. *Neuroscience & Biobehavioral Reviews, 43,* 48-73. https://doi.org/10.1016/j.neubiorev.2014.03.016

Gardner, T. J. (2007). Speech recognition for students with disabilities in writing. *Journal of Special Education Technology, 22*(2), 31-38. https://files.eric.ed.gov/fulltext/EJ795377.pdf

Gere, D. R., Capps, S. C., Mitchell, D. W., & Grubbs, E. (2009). Sensory sensitivities of gifted children. *The American Journal of Occupational Therapy, 63*(3), 288-295. https://doi.org/10.5014/ajot.63.3.288

Gurung, R. A. R., & Landrum, R. E. (2014). *Using evidence-based teaching methods to promote social and emotional skills in students.* Jossey-Bass.

Hölzel, B. K., Carmody, J., Vangel, M., Congleton, C., Yerramsetti, S. M., Gard, T., & Lazar, S. W. (2011). Mindfulness practice leads to increases in regional brain gray matter density. *Psychiatry Research: Neuroimaging, 191*(1), 36-43. https://doi.org/10.1016/j.pscychresns.2010.08.006

Jarrard, P. (2023). Sensory issues in gifted children. STAR Institute for Sensory Processing Disorder. https://sensoryhealth.org/sites/default/files/publications/SensoryissuesinGiftedChildren.pdf

Karimova, H. (2017, December 24). The emotion wheel: What it is and how to use it. *PositivePsychology.com.* https://positivepsychology.com/emotion-wheel/

Killgore, W. D. S., et al. (2017). Emotional intensity and sensitivity in twice-exceptional students: A cognitive perspective. *Neuroscience of Emotion, 34*(2), 123-136.

Krohn, M. D. (2007). The nature of emotions: Fundamental questions and implications for emotional intelligence. *Review of Psychology, 58*(3), 193-214.

Lee, I. X. C. (2011). *The application of speech recognition technology for remediating the writing difficulties of students with learning disabilities* (Publication No. 3501541) [Doctoral dissertation, University of Washington]. ProQuest Dissertations and Theses Global.

Lovecky, D. V. (2023). Emotional characteristics of gifted and twice-exceptional learners. *Gifted Child Quarterly, 67*(2), 105-116.

MacArthur, C. A., & Cavalier, A. R. (2004). Dictation and speech recognition technology as test accommodations. *Exceptional Children, 71*(1), 43-58. https://doi.org/10.1177/001440290407100103

Maxwell, K., & Gurin, P. (2017). Using dialogue to create inclusive classrooms: A case study from a faculty institute. *Liberal Education, 103*(3-4), 10-15.

Pekrun, R., & Linnenbrink-Garcia, L. (Eds.). (2014). *International Handbook of Emotions in Education*. Routledge. https://doi.org/10.4324/9780203148211

Peterson, J. S. (2019). Promoting effective group work among 2e students. *Gifted Child Today*, 42(3), 165–172.

Plutchik, R. (1961). Studies of emotion in the light of a new theory. *Psychological Reports, 8*(1), 170–176. https://journals.sagepub.com/doi/full/10.2466/pr0.1961.8.1.170

Plutchik, R. (2001). The nature of emotions. *American Scientist, 89*(4), 344–350. https://www.emotionalcompetency.com/papers/plutchiknatureofemotions%202001.pdf

Plutchik, R. (2007). The emotions: Facts, theories, and a new model. American Scientist.

Reis, S. M., Baum, S. M., & Burke, E. (2014). An operational definition of twice-exceptional learners: Implications and applications. *Gifted Child Quarterly, 58*(3), 217–230. https://doi.org/10.1177/0016986214534976

Ramírez, D., Guzman-Lavín, E. J., Pulgar, J., & Candia, C. (2023). *Affinity-based groups in secondary education: Increased stability at the expense of collaboration*. arXiv. https://arxiv.org/abs/2309.15212

Roeckelein, J. E. (2006). Elsevier's dictionary of psychological theories. Elsevier. Screenr, C. (2017). Emotional responses and survival behaviors in education. Education and Survival *Psychology Quarterly, 39*(4), 67–78.

Sisk, D. A. (2021). Managing the emotional intensities of gifted students with mindfulness practices. *Education Sciences, 11*(11), 731. https://doi.org/10.3390/educsci11110731

Tang, Y. Y., Hölzel, B. K., & Posner, M. I. (2015). The neuroscience of mindfulness meditation. *Nature Reviews Neuroscience, 16*(4), 213–225. https://doi.org/10.1038/nrn3916

Zenner, C., Herrnleben-Kurz, S., & Walach, H. (2014). Mindfulness-based interventions in schools—a systematic review and meta-analysis. *Frontiers in Psychology, 5*, 603. https://doi.org/10.3389/fpsyg.2014.00603

CHAPTER 7
Brilliant Brains
Nina Thomas

Neurodiversity, the concept that neurological differences are to be recognised and respected as any other human variation, is central to creating inclusive educational environments (Baum et al., 2017). This approach celebrates the unique ways individuals with diverse neurological conditions, such as those who are twice-exceptional (2e), perceive and interact with the world. Embracing neurodiversity in educational settings not only fosters acceptance and understanding but also enhances the learning experiences of all students by leveraging their unique strengths.

Recognising and valuing individual differences

Twice-exceptional learners face unique challenges in traditional educational environments. These students possess remarkable talents and intellectual abilities while also grappling with difficulties that can hinder their academic and social success. Celebrating neurodiversity means recognising these dual characteristics and implementing supportive practices that address both their exceptional strengths and areas of need (Park & Galloway, 2024). To truly support twice-exceptional students, educators must embrace teaching strategies that cater to their diverse cognitive profiles.

A key component in supporting neurodivergent students, particularly twice-exceptional learners, is the use of scaffolded practice in teaching.

Research by Jarrod Horvath highlights scaffolded practice as a powerful method for enhancing memory and promoting long-term retention, making it especially effective for twice-exceptional students. This strategy involves breaking down complex tasks into smaller, more manageable steps and providing appropriate support until students gain independence.

Horvath's (2019) research underscores the benefits of scaffolded practice in fostering robust memory formation and retention, which is particularly beneficial for twice-exceptional learners who may excel cognitively yet face specific learning challenges (Horvath, 2022). By leveraging the brain's capacity for neuroplasticity – the ability to form new neural connections – educators can tailor scaffolded practices to meet the unique needs of these students, ensuring their exceptional abilities are nurtured while addressing their learning difficulties (Reis & Renzulli, 2011).

The role of neuroplasticity

Neuroplasticity refers to the brain's remarkable ability to adapt and change in response to experiences and learning (Puderbaugh & Emmady, 2023). Scaffolded practice takes advantage of this by providing structured, incremental support that helps students gradually build and strengthen neural pathways (Reis & Renzulli, 2011). This ensures that learning is not only retained in the short term but also reinforced for future recall and application. Scaffolded instruction involves progressively increasing the complexity of tasks, allowing students to build on their skills step by step (Baum et al., 2017). By engaging the brain in repeated practice through gradually more challenging activities, neural connections are continuously strengthened.

For example, in a math class, students might begin with basic arithmetic problems. As they gain proficiency, they progress to more complex calculations that require multiple steps. At each stage, their brains actively encode and reinforce this new information, deepening their understanding (Tai et al., 2021). This scaffolded approach ensures that knowledge is effectively transferred from short-term to long-term memory, providing a solid foundation for future recall (Reis & Renzulli, 2011).

This systematic reinforcement is particularly beneficial for twice-exceptional learners, who often exhibit advanced cognitive abilities alongside specific learning challenges (Baum et al., 2017). Scaffolded practice supports their cognitive strengths while simultaneously addressing their learning needs, enabling them to fully engage with the material, retain information, and apply their knowledge when needed (Keesey & Highbaugh, 2018).

Example of enhancing long-term retention

Case study: Dion

Dion, a twice-exceptional student, possesses advanced intellectual abilities but also faces learning challenges that require specific support strategies. His learning needs include structured guidance to break down complex information into manageable parts, active engagement through hands-on activities, and continuous feedback to help him reflect and improve. Dion benefits from visual aids and technology to organise and retain information and requires gradual scaffolding to build autonomy in his learning. Additionally, he needs a learning environment that embraces mistakes as growth opportunities and incorporates spaced practice to enhance long-term retention (Kennette & Wilson, 2019).

Scaffolded Strategy	Description	Application in Dion's Case
Segmenting complex information	Breaking down complex concepts into manageable parts and building upon them incrementally.	Dion's teacher breaks down the concept of ecosystems into smaller sections, starting with basic components (producers, consumers, decomposers) before moving to complex interactions.
Active engagement and modelling	Engaging students by modelling tasks and providing guided practice.	The teacher models setting up a terrarium to observe ecosystem components. Dion practices with guidance, helping him fully engage with each step.
Continuous feedback and reflection	Providing ongoing feedback and encouraging self-reflection to deepen understanding.	Dion receives feedback after each experiment and keeps a learning journal to reflect on challenges and successful strategies.

Scaffolded Strategy	Description	Application in Dion's Case
Utilising visual aids and technology	Using visual tools and technology to support understanding and retention.	Concept maps visually represent ecosystems, and interactive simulations allow Dion to explore different ecosystems virtually, reinforcing his learning.
Gradual release of responsibility	Slowly reducing teacher support, encouraging students to take more responsibility for their learning.	The teacher initially provides detailed instructions, then gradually allows Dion to design his own experiments, fostering autonomy.
Embracing errors as learning opportunities	Framing mistakes as valuable learning moments to build resilience and confidence.	The teacher encourages Dion to view mistakes as learning opportunities, reducing anxiety and fostering a deeper understanding of the material.
Incorporating active recall and practice spacing	Using regular reviews and spaced practice sessions to enhance retention.	Dion regularly reviews key concepts through quizzes and spaced practice exercises, leveraging the spacing effect to improve memory retention.

By employing scaffolded practices – such as segmenting information, providing active engagement, using visual aids, offering continuous feedback, gradually releasing responsibility, embracing errors, and incorporating spaced practice – Dion's teacher helps him not only understand the complex concepts of ecosystems but also retain and apply the knowledge effectively. These strategies ensure that Dion's long-term retention and application of the material are reinforced, enabling him to thrive both academically and in practical settings.

Building a culture of acceptance and support

Many schools struggle with where to start to support 2e students. By implementing the following strategies, educators can create a holistic and inclusive learning environment where twice-exceptional learners can thrive. The focus on emotional intelligence, scaffolded learning, and community engagement ensures that neurodiversity is celebrated, and every student has the opportunity to reach their full potential (Gierczyk & Hornby, 2021).

Strategy	Description	Implementation
Inclusive policies and practices	Develop school policies that explicitly support neurodivergent students, ensuring access to resources and accommodations.	Flexible deadlines, alternative assessments, access to assistive technologies, and tailored learning plans for neurodivergent students.
Family and community engagement	Engage families and the broader community in the educational process to create a consistent support system.	Provide resources and support for families, host informational sessions, and encourage family participation in school activities.
Professional development for educators	Continuous training to help educators understand and implement best practices for supporting neurodivergent students.	Workshops, seminars, and collaborative learning communities to enhance teachers' skills in addressing the needs of twice-exceptional learners.
Student voice and choice	Empower neurodivergent students by allowing them to make choices in their learning, increasing engagement and ownership.	Offer options for learning paths, projects, and assessments, fostering student autonomy and self-advocacy.

Celebrating diversity through curriculum	Integrate themes of diversity and neurodiversity into the curriculum to foster understanding and appreciation of all learners.	Include diverse perspectives in literature, history, and social studies, and highlight contributions from neurodivergent individuals.
Scaffolded learning practices	Use scaffolded practices to support memory and retention, leveraging neuroplasticity to enhance learning.	Apply Jarrod Horvath's model to break down tasks, use repetition, and gradually increase complexity to reinforce learning.
Emotions as catalysts for growth	Recognise emotions as powerful signals for personal growth, resilience, and social connection.	Teach emotional intelligence, encourage self-awareness, and use emotions as learning tools to build resilience and adaptability.
Resilience and adaptability	Encourage the constructive management of emotions like disappointment or frustration to foster resilience and growth.	Teach strategies for managing difficult emotions and turning challenges into opportunities for personal development.
Social connections and support	Emphasise the role of emotions in forming supportive social connections, crucial for emotional wellbeing and growth.	Foster positive social interactions, provide opportunities for peer collaboration, and build a network of support within the school community.

The Differentiated Model of Giftedness and Talented

The DMGT, widely adopted in Australia and other educational contexts, provides a comprehensive framework for understanding and fostering talent development. Developed by educational psychologist Françoys

Gagné (2004; 2013; 2015), this model outlines how innate abilities (gifts) can be developed into systematically developed skills (talents) through a process influenced by various environmental and personal factors (Gagné, 2004; 2013).

Figure 1: The Differentiated Model of Giftedness and Talented (DMGT)

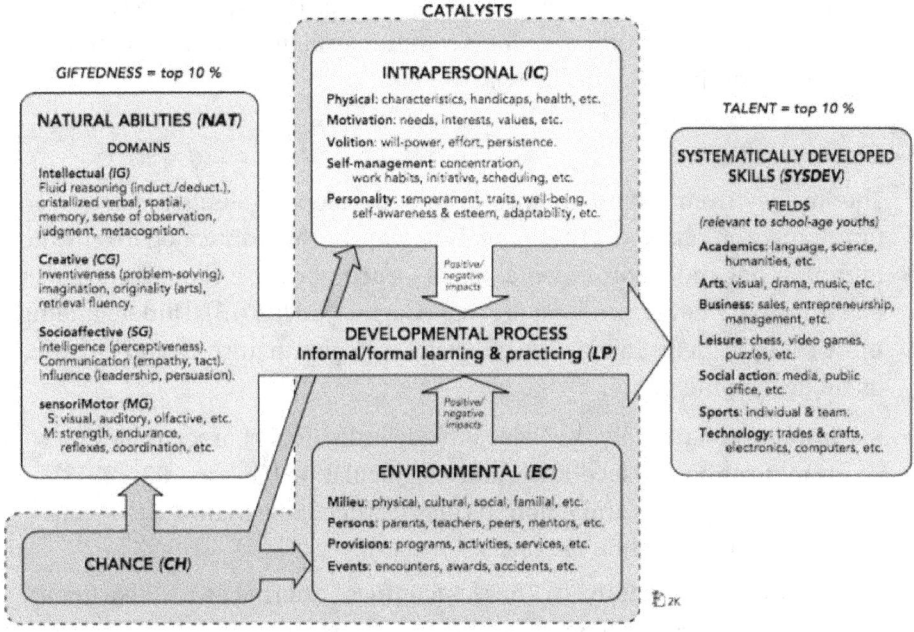

Gagné's Differentiated Model of Giftedness and Talent (DMGT.EN.2K)

IMAGE SOURCE: HTTP://WWW.CURRICULUMSUPPORT.EDUCATION.NSW.GOV.AU/POLICIES/GATS/ASSETS/PDF/POLDMGTCOLRDIAG.PDF

Key components of the Gagné model

Gagné's DMGT (2004; 2015) outlines the essential components that distinguish natural abilities from developed talents. This model emphasises the importance of recognising and nurturing inherent aptitudes while systematically fostering these abilities through structured development processes (Gagné, 2004). Understanding these key components provides a framework for effectively identifying and cultivating giftedness and talent.

- **Natural abilities (gifts):** According to Gagné (2004; 2015), gifts are natural abilities or aptitudes in specific domains, such as intellectual, creative, social, perceptual, or motor skills. These are the raw potentials that individuals are born with, which can be identified and if nurtured, can turn into talents.
- **Systematic development (talents):** Talents are systematically developed skills or competencies that result from the transformation of natural abilities through learning, practice, and experience (Gagné, 2013). This development process requires structured and sustained effort over time (Gagné, 2004).

Catalysts

The journey from innate abilities to fully developed talents is influenced by a range of catalysts. These catalysts can be broadly categorised into intrapersonal and environmental factors, each playing a significant role in an individual's developmental process (Gagné, 2004; 2013). Understanding these catalysts helps in creating effective strategies to nurture and enhance talent development.

- **Intrapersonal catalysts:** These include individual characteristics such as motivation, perseverance, and self-regulation (Gagné, 2004; 2013). Personal attitudes and emotions play a crucial role in how effectively one can develop their talents.
- **Environmental catalysts:** These encompass external factors like family support, educational opportunities, mentors, and cultural influences (Gagné, 2013). A nurturing and enriching environment is essential for talent development.
- **Developmental process:** The transformation from natural abilities to developed talents involves a dynamic interaction between intrapersonal and environmental catalysts. This process includes formal and informal learning experiences, deliberate practice, feedback, and support (Gagné, 2004).

Passion and opportunity in the Gagné Model

The DMGT underscores the vital importance of passion and opportunity in the journey from natural abilities to fully developed talents. It highlights how innate gifts can be transformed into talents through a dynamic interplay of various catalysts, driven by an individual's enthusiasm and the opportunities available to them (Gagné, 2013; 2021). Understanding this interplay is crucial for fostering talent development effectively.

Passion: The driving force behind talent development

Passion serves as a powerful internal catalyst that fuels an individual's motivation and persistence (Gagné, 2013). It is the deep, intrinsic interest and enthusiasm that drives a person to engage deeply with a particular domain. Passion leads to sustained effort, resilience in the face of challenges, and a commitment to continuous improvement. For twice-exceptional (2e) learners, who may face unique challenges in traditional educational settings, passion can be a crucial element that keeps them engaged and motivated despite potential obstacles.

For example: Consider a 2e student who has exceptional mathematical abilities. Their passion for solving complex mathematical problems can drive them to focus intensely on this area, spending hours exploring mathematical theories and solving challenging problems. This passion helps them navigate social and sensory challenges associated with their exceptionalities, channelling their energy into productive and fulfilling activities.

Opportunity: The essential external catalyst

Opportunity, as highlighted by the DMGT (Gagné, 2004; 2021), represents the external factors and environments that enable the development of talent. These include access to resources, exposure to challenging and enriching experiences, supportive mentors, and a conducive learning environment (Gagné, 2013). Opportunities provide the necessary scaffolding that allows individuals to practise, refine, and showcase their abilities, transforming their innate gifts into well-developed talents.

For example: A 2e student with a passion for computer programming may benefit significantly from opportunities such as advanced coding classes, participation in programming competitions, access to state-of-the-art technology, and mentorship from experienced programmers. These opportunities enable the student to apply their passion in meaningful ways, receive feedback, and grow their skills in a supportive environment that accommodates their unique needs.

The synergy of passion and opportunity

The synergy between passion and opportunity is essential for the full realisation of potential. While passion drives individuals to pursue their interests relentlessly, opportunities provide the pathways and platforms for this pursuit to be structured and fruitful (Gagné, 2004; 2021). For 2e students, this synergy can be particularly transformative as it allows them to leverage their unique strengths while receiving the support they need to overcome their challenges, thereby fostering both their exceptional abilities and addressing their learning differences in a cohesive manner.

For example, consider a school that implements a specialised program for twice-exceptional (2e) students, designed to identify and nurture their unique strengths. A student with a passion for robotics might be given the opportunity to engage in real-world projects, participate in robotics workshops, and collaborate with peers who share similar interests. This alignment of the student's passion for robotics with the opportunities provided by the school's program allows the student to excel, fostering the creation of innovative robotic solutions and potentially paving the way for a future career in engineering.

In summary, the DMGT (Gagné, 2004; 2015; 2021) emphasis on passion and opportunity underscores the importance of both internal and external catalysts in the development of talent. For educators, a deep understanding and strategic use of these elements can lead to more effective methods for nurturing the potential of all students. This approach not only enhances educational outcomes but also promotes a paradigm shift in how we perceive and support exceptionalities, fostering greater acceptance of neurodiversity and recognising the diverse strengths and unique needs of each learner. By encouraging passion and providing opportunities, educators can significantly impact the holistic development of their students, particularly those who are twice exceptional.

 **KEY TAKEAWAYS**

- **Embracing neurodiversity:** Neurodiversity recognises neurological differences as natural variations of the human experience. Celebrating neurodiversity in education fosters an inclusive environment, supporting twice-exceptional (2e) students by recognising and leveraging their unique strengths and addressing their challenges.

- **The power of scaffolded learning and neuroplasticity:** Scaffolded learning strategies, supported by neuroplasticity research, help 2e learners build cognitive pathways for long-term retention. Breaking down complex tasks and gradually increasing their complexity enables these students to capitalise on their intellectual abilities while addressing learning challenges.

- **The role of passion and opportunity:** According to Gagné's Differentiated Model of Giftedness and Talent (DMGT), passion and opportunity are essential for transforming innate abilities into talents. For 2e students, aligning their interests with structured opportunities enhances engagement, resilience, and skill development.

- **Creating inclusive policies and practices:** Effective support for neurodivergent learners requires inclusive educational policies, professional development for teachers, tailored learning plans, and family engagement. These strategies create a supportive framework for neurodiverse learners to thrive.

- **Cultivating emotional intelligence and resilience:** Developing emotional intelligence and resilience in 2e students helps them navigate the challenges of dual exceptionalities. Teaching self-awareness, emotional regulation, and constructive management of setbacks fosters their personal growth, confidence, and social connections.

Chapter references

Baum, S. M., Schader, R. M., & Owen, S. V. (2017). *To be gifted and learning disabled: Strength-based strategies for helping twice-exceptional students with LD, ADHD, ASD, and more.* Prufrock Press.

Gagné, F. (2004). Transforming gifts into talents: The DMGT as a developmental theory. *High Ability Studies, 15*(2), 119–147.

Gagné, F. (2013). The DMGT: Changes within, beneath, and beyond. *Talent Development & Excellence, 5*(1), 5–19.

Gagné, F. (2015). From gifts to talents: The DMGT as a developmental model. In R. F. Subotnik, A. Olszewski-Kubilius, & F. C. Worrell (Eds.), *The psychology of high performance: Developing human potential into domain-specific talent* (pp. 83–104). American Psychological Association.

Gagné, F. (2021). *Understanding giftedness: A guide for parents and educators.* Routledge.

Gierczyk, M., & Hornby, G. (2021). Twice-exceptional students: Review of implications for special and inclusive education. *Education Sciences, 11*(2), 77

Horvath, J. C. (2019). *Stop talking, start influencing: 12 insights from brain science to make your message stick.* Exisle Publishing.

Horvath, J. C. (2022). The Learning Blueprint - Science of Learning PD. LME Global. Retrieved from https://www.lmeglobal.net/the-learning-blueprint

Keesey, S., & Highbaugh, K. (2018). Using high-leverage practices to support twice-exceptional learners. *Kentucky Teacher Education Journal, 5*(1), Article 5. https://doi.org/10.61611/2995-5904.1009

Kennette, L. N., & Wilson, N. A. (2019). Universal Design for Learning (UDL): Student and faculty perceptions. J*ournal of Effective Teaching in Higher Education, 2*(1), 70–76. https://doi.org/10.36021/jethe.v2i1.17

Park, H.-J., & Galloway, L. (2024). Who are twice-exceptional students? R*eview of Disability Studies: An International Journal, 20*(1). https://rdsjournal.org/index.php/journal/article/view/1357

Puderbaugh, M., & Emmady, P. D. (2023, May 1). Neuroplasticity. In *StatPearls*. StatPearls Publishing.

Reis, S. M., & Renzulli, J. S. (2011). Challenging gifted and talented learners with a continuum of research-based intervention strategies. In M. A. Bray & T. J. Kehle (Eds.), *The Oxford handbook of school psychology* (pp. 456–482). Oxford University Press.

Tai, H.-C., Chen, C.-M., Tsai, Y.-H., Lee, B.-O., & Dewi, Y. S. (2021). Is instructional scaffolding a better strategy for teaching writing to EFL learners? A functional MRI study in healthy young adults. *Brain Sciences, 11*(11), 1378. https://doi.org/10.3390/brainsci11111378

CHAPTER 8
Building Bridges – The Home and School Partnership
Geraldine Nicholas

School can be a difficult place for so many young people however when there is a learning disability and a gifted diagnosis, this can become an even greater challenge for all involved. For so many, building that community of support is the key to success in navigating the game of 'school'.

This chapter will look at how schools can build trust and honour the learning and social emotional needs of the individual student. Both families and school need to work together and manage the many challenges that every neurodivergent child has. Parents are the first to notice, identify and advocate for their child. Therapists help manage, support and assist both the child and family to understand the challenges that are faced and encourage proactivity in getting the support that is required. Schools need to develop an environment where the stakeholders in any child's education are listened to and welcomed.

My journey in understanding the 2e child has been long, sometimes fraught with not knowing but always making sure that everyone talks and shares. For me, so much is based on knowing the child, and understanding their particular needs.

Understanding twice-exceptional students: Case studies and insights

I want to first share with you the story of one student. Let's call him George. George had been diagnosed with Autism and ADHD. The transition from kindergarten to primary as well as the early years of primary school were challenging. Behavioural issues started to arise in years 2 and 3. George was given an Individual Learning Plan (ILP) that sought to meet his high academic needs but the ILP failed. Psychological support was made available and with effective pastoral assistance, adjustments were made, and George began to flourish. As George's mum stated, part of the effectiveness of the plan was the delivery of professional learning which broke down the barriers, ensuring that teachers understood that being gifted with learning disabilities was not unusual.

Targeted professional learning meant that perceptions were broken down, understanding was built and inclusive adjustments could be made. Thus, for George and other students at this school, a more effective learning environment was being built. The move to secondary school was still full of challenges however the welcoming environment, educational adjustments and proactive leadership and teaching staff made this move less traumatic. The fact that school and home were always in communication enabled overcoming any challenge relatively easy. For George, feeling a part of the school community as well as being placed within the gifted cohort brought out the best in him. The opportunity to participate in extracurricular programs such as Tournament of Minds, Ethics Olympiad, chess and debating gave him a further sense of belonging.

Another case study to share is Beth. Beth is an alert, highly capable yet anxious young person. She has an ASD high functioning diagnosis, a lower processing speed meaning that she needs time to process information, especially new knowledge, yet has well-advanced potential for learning. Beth is social and has a great group of friends, she enjoys many aspects of school including sport. When confronted with new content, Beth can require time to process; asks many questions to clarify and time is needed to practice and embed information especially with maths.

Both George and Beth are representative of gifted and learning disabled or 2e students. Their history is important as is understanding their strengths to ensure that strengths are seen above deficits. For me, addressing the "what" of each student and working with families to ensure regular contact and information sharing takes place enables the bridge to be built so that success occurs. For every 2e student, their learning challenge matters as it is a lifelong "disability". For some, it can become like a superpower and for others it can be totally disabling. Learning to manage and to thrive despite "it" is essential. To feel safe, valued and accepted is paramount.

Building effective learning plans and educational support systems

School is a place where the curriculum, instruction and enrichment opportunities need to be ongoing. They inform the services that are available as well as the interventions that may be necessary to reduce the impact of the deficits. For me, the focus is on finding and targeting what a student's strengths are and to develop a talent development mindset as without attention to the ability that every student possesses, we are in danger of providing a restrictive environment that does not seek to meet their individual needs.

Curriculum and delivery of knowledge needs a special mention here. Great curriculum that which aligns to the needs and readiness of the student. June Maker and Carol Ann Tomlinson constantly call for teachers to know where their students are in their learning and to furnish differentiation where the content, process and product allows each young person to meet where they are at, to be challenge just beyond their comfort zone and to show what they have understood. For the gifted student, challenge ensures that cognitive engagement in school is developed so that students are as invested in their learning as much as the teachers who have planned for the learning.

The skill of "learning how to learn" is especially relevant as these skills must be taught and constantly reinforced for our 2e students. The strain of asynchronous development means that their executive functioning is an area that can be years behind their peers' ability. Here with the aid of a targeted learning plan and support from psychologists, skills can be grown and the impact of deficits reduced. Thus, the use of Individual Learning Plans or Support Plans with targeted goals, supported by proactive learning staff and advocating families can work together to ensure that the school experience is overwhelmingly positive.

So, how can the sometimes divergent parts – school and home – of a child's life come together to ensure that the same vision is being seen? As already hinted, home is where the child was first noticed. Parents are the child's first educators; they know the history and have often shared the pain and joy of the 2e individual. They have faced frustrations, lack of knowledge, hurdles and sometimes endless medical appointments. They have told their story a multitude of times. Primarily, they want the best for their child and ensuring that occurs can be a tricky path. The relationship between school and home needs to be mutually respectful and supportive. There needs to be understanding of the protocols that exist within a school and the chain of command. Both sides need to build trust, open lines of communication and be ready to compromise. Alternatives need to discussed as well as an understanding of what is available as not all schools are blessed with a highly resourced and competent learning services program or staff.

So, what can be done at home and school to make stakeholders aware of the journey that the child needs to flourish? For many schools, that starts with an educational plan. There are many titles – Individual Learning Plan, Individual Educational Plan and Student Support Plan (See Chapter 3) are among the most common. Irrespective of the title, the idea is to set a plan in place that will allow the student to develop their strengths and reduce the impact of their deficits. A strengths-based approach should be the preferred model where a multi-tiered systems of supports (MTSS) is brought together so that there are multiple points of assessment or data and evidence/information gathered. Additionally, there should be an emphasis on a positive educational outcome with goals set and reviewed in a timely and continuous manner. The inclusion of SMART goals as previously covered are a non-negotiable as they allow data and information to be constantly gathered to inform the learning and thus the teaching.

The Learning Plan is one that everyone needs to contribute to. Parent/s and students need to discuss what they need from the school and schools need to be able to put into place resources and time to develop the plan. At home, open communication between parent/s and the child can be confronting especially during the secondary years. Goals can be multi-faceted including academic as well as social emotional goals. Expectations for many aspects of a program including exam conditions, learning adjustments, use of learning assistants and technology, participation in camps, co-curricular and extra-curricular activities can be included. Additionally appointments including respite plans and visits from speech therapists and occupational therapists can all be included. The inclusion of as many aspects of a student's life at school will assist everyone to be open and transparent and to trust the process.

Once goals have been shared and set, timely reviews need to be communicated. The reviews should ideally depend on the level of support that is required. It goes without saying that the higher the needs of the student, the more frequent the meetings and communication. Ideally, most unicorns should have their plans reviewed and adjusted once a term, but at a minimum once a semester. This needs to be outside the 7-10 min parent, teacher, student conferences. Once agreed upon, the plan needs to be available for all teaching staff so that information can be shared, and the targeted learning can occur. With the presence of well-developed and informative plans, teachers can effectively differentiate the curriculum so that the level of readiness, content and instruction is best suited to the student.

Teachers also need to ensure that they have within their repertoire of teaching strategies a highly developed and informed approach by using the best differentiated teaching practices available. Being informed means that teachers are continually kept abreast of what is current, informed by evidence and willing to experiment and go beyond their comfort zone so that the child is given the opportunity to "learn one new thing every day". School based professional learning like the type George's teachers were exposed to ensures that the frustrations parent/s and students experience are reduced. It is also worthwhile reminding all stakeholders that the social emotional needs of the student should be included within the plan.

The difficulty for many teachers is implementing the individual learning needs that psychologist and other professionals recommend. The best interest of the child does not always align with the practicalities that teachers face on a daily basis. There are often generalised recommendations that become a standard of many independent learning plans.

Practical strategies for implementing recommendations

Some strategies of how to apply the recommendation of learning needs in the classroom are outlined below:

Recommendation	Primary Education Implementation	Secondary Education Implementation
Differentiated instruction	Use tiered activities that cater to various skill levels; provide different levels of text complexity and tasks.	Offer choice boards or contracts where students select from a range of activities or assignments tailored to their needs.
Flexible grouping	Group students by similar ability levels for certain tasks or projects; rotate groups regularly to expose students to diverse peer interactions.	Use interest-based or ability-based groups for projects; adjust groupings based on ongoing assessments and feedback.
Individualised Learning Plans (ILPs)	Develop ILPs with specific goals and strategies tailored to each student's needs; involve parents in setting and reviewing goals.	Create ILPs that include academic and behavioural goals, and review progress with students regularly to adjust strategies.
Use of assistive technology	Integrate tools such as text-to-speech software or interactive learning apps to support diverse learning needs.	Employ advanced tools such as speech recognition software or specialised educational apps for research and writing tasks.
Formative assessments	Conduct regular check-ins and use informal assessments like quizzes, exit tickets, or observational notes to gauge understanding.	Use quizzes, self-assessments, and peer assessments to provide ongoing feedback and adjust instruction as needed.

Recommendation	Primary Education Implementation	Secondary Education Implementation
Scaffolded learning	Break tasks into smaller, manageable steps; provide guided practice with gradual release of responsibility. Use visual prompts to support the verbal instructions.	Provide scaffolds like outlines, templates, or graphic organisers; offer step-by-step support and then gradually reduce assistance.
Enrichment opportunities	Offer extension activities or challenge tasks for advanced learners; use centres or stations with advanced material.	Provide opportunities for independent research, advanced coursework, or mentorship programs to explore areas of interest.
Collaborative learning	Facilitate group projects and peer tutoring; use cooperative learning structures to build social and academic skills.	Encourage collaboration through group assignments, debates, or peer review processes, fostering both teamwork and individual contribution.
Rest breaks	Scheduled brain breaks and use of timers to help organise activities.	Implementation of a system where students can take a 'walk' guided meditation, where there is no consequence, but the break is timed digitally or manually.

 **KEY TAKEAWAYS**

- **Building trust between school and home:** Developing a strong partnership between families and schools is critical for supporting 2e students. Parents are the first advocates for their child, while schools must provide an inclusive environment that fosters collaboration and communication with families to build trust and ensure shared goals.

- **Strength-based and individualised approaches:** A strengths-based approach, supported by Individual Learning Plans (ILPs) or Student Support Plans, allows schools to address the unique needs of 2e students by focusing on their abilities while implementing strategies to minimise their challenges.

- **Effective professional learning:** Targeted professional learning for teachers improves their understanding of twice-exceptional learners and equips them with evidence-based strategies to support academic, social-emotional, and behavioural needs. This leads to more inclusive and effective classroom practices.

- **Differentiated and scaffolded instruction:** Teachers must employ differentiated instruction, scaffolded learning, and assistive technologies to meet the needs of 2e students. These strategies ensure that students are working within their 'zone of proximal development', maintaining both challenge and support.

- **Regular review and adaptation of plans:** Frequent and structured reviews of learning plans, involving parents, teachers, and students, ensure that the strategies remain relevant and effective. Continuous communication and adjustments based on feedback are essential for fostering growth and progress.

Chapter references

Maker, J. (2005). *Curriculum development for gifted students.* Austin, TX: Pro-Ed.

Tomlinson, C. A. (2017). *The differentiated classroom: Responding to the needs of all learners* (2nd ed.). ASCD.

Australian Government Department of Education. (2024). *Guidelines for Individual Learning Plans.* Canberra: Commonwealth of Australia.

CHAPTER 9
Thinking Differently is His Superpower: CASE STUDY Billy

Mark Smith

Understanding twice-exceptional students: Characteristics and challenges

Having led large, multi-faceted gifted and talented programs in multiple schools for almost two decades, I have seen my share of twice-exceptional students. Reis et al. (2014) refers to these individuals as possessing exceptional potential or achievement in one or more academic domains, but also holding a significant disability inhibiting their expression of potential or ability. The disability could be associated with their learning, language, speech, social/emotional regulation, their physical ability, attention deficit or autism spectrum. These students present in many unique and sometimes quirky ways which may include being:

- Highly able creatively and artistically but inhibited by processing skills and/or work ethic.
- Highly able mathematically, algorithmically and quantitatively, but inhibited by auditory processing and/or literacy skills.
- Highly able visually in a range of disciplines but inhibited by processing speed and/or working memory.

- Highly able with abstract problem solving and thinking outside the box, deeply and critically, yet inhibited by basic executive functioning and/or social skills.
- Highly able with superior development in thinking and strategy but inhibited by immaturity in their growth and/or personal development.

Indeed, twice-exceptional students have just as many differences, quirks and anomalies as many other student groups.

For educators, our goals remain the same. To enable these students to be their best selves and to achieve according to their capabilities. The challenge with twice-exceptional students is to uncover the mask, or cognitive challenge that inhibits their academic and personal growth, enabling these students to show their exceptional abilities and to thrive in work and in life.

Case studies are an interesting and helpful way to look at these students. To firstly consider their learner profile, to then think about the challenges they face and work with purpose to address them, and finally to learn from how the challenge was successfully overcome and consider how the learning program will be sustained.

There are many strategies that could be applied to such students, but each individual is unique, and it is critical to be sensitive to the needs and learning challenges of each student case by case. Trail (2022) encourages those that work with twice-exceptional students to help them develop a growth mindset, where they are encouraged not to see their personal development as fixed, but rather to see their mistakes or shortfalls as learning opportunities. Lessons to learn from as they grow and develop.

Having worked in the gifted field for so many years I have learned much from my reading, deliberations with colleagues, efforts in process, and actions taken. This work has always been done in the best interest of my students, and over time I have developed a degree of wisdom from the challenges and the successes.

Billy's journey: A case study

Billy came to my school at the start of year 5. For the first few days he spent considerable time in isolation at the back of the room or under a desk. He was not disruptive, but he was on edge in his new setting. The teacher was supportive and understanding, giving him space and encouraging him to be more involved as was appropriate. The teacher checked in with Billy regularly and worked hard to build rapport. Other students in the class went about their role without drama. They were not sidetracked or impacted by Billy's presence but their interaction with him was limited. Billy spent lunch time and recess on his own, or talking to the teacher on yard duty. Sometimes he read a book as he loved to read.

Building the learning profile

In those first few weeks the Learning Support Department was aware of Billy, but they monitored his progress encouraging his teacher to support him to find his place in the classroom. Those working with Billy knew that a sense of belonging was critical for him to show his true self. They also did some research to find out what other information could be found about Billy and his history, but very little was available other than his school reports which were very general.

As term 1 progressed Billy started to complete work in class. All was addressed at a basic level and no homework was done, but Billy was progressing. Soon after, to gain a greater snapshot of Billy's ability, an Australian Council for Educational Research, ACER (2019) General Ability Test (AGAT) was completed with Billy. His results fell into the average range for the Numeracy and Verbal domains, but Billy did score 100% in the Abstract thinking domain. This abstract thinking result was surprising and unexpected, but we acknowledged that it was just one test and more exploration was needed.

So very early we were beginning to establish that Billy loved reading, we had also established through one test that he was probably a high-level thinker. So, his teacher began to work to further encourage his reading and thinking skills.

Billy's deficits were also beginning to express themselves. From day one we were aware that socially Billy was highly challenged, and it soon became evident that his executive functioning, and general organisation was well below what was expected for a student of his age.

Developing a strengths-based approach

With a profile of Billy starting to emerge the teacher was encouraged to firstly work to Billy's strengths. Well-founded research in the field, including shared advice in Baum et al. (2021) encourages a strengths-based learning approach with twice-exceptional students, as history has told us that working to these strengths is a positive approach to supporting a student that can be so inhibited by their deficits. Focusing on the student's strengths first acknowledges their abilities and demonstrates belief in the student which can build confidence and stoicism.

Though Billy had not been formally assessed, the Learning Support team suspected that Billy was likely on the autism spectrum. Triggers such as loud, unexpected noises, or a change of daily routine were negatively impacting Billy through stress and anxiety in the classroom, confirming the likely autism spectrum belief. This combined with Billy's social and organisational deficits, but also his superior thinking skills, his aptitude for technology, and his insatiable passion for reading led us to suspect very early that he was probably a twice-exceptional child.

By encouraging Billy's reading, the teacher established his areas of passion and interest, and wherever possible he fed those passions with books that he intuitively believed Billy would like, including books on justice and ethics, and books focusing on technological fields including animation, game making and film. By the middle of term 2 Billy was reading books that were in the senior secondary age range according to his passions. Consequently, his knowledge, and in some cases his practical skills were growing in these areas of interest as a result. The teacher also found that Billy's reading strength was starting to support his English work as he started to delve into more advanced books in English.

Billy was becoming a prolific reader, with every spare moment at school translating to another reading opportunity. When it came to writing about what he was reading Billy was ahead of the game in terms of knowledge because he had read so much on the topic. His knowledge was providing confidence as Billy was now often willing to share some of what he was learning from his reading during class discussions, sometimes astounding his classmates with his knowledge.

On one occasion early in term 3 Billy shared his extraordinary knowledge regarding the current English text. In answer to the teacher's question, Billy shared not only what he had read and understood from the text directly, but he shared his inferred feelings about the text from a justice perspective which was so profound his classmates physically applauded his two-minute answer.

Not only was Billy's confidence growing from his reading skills and knowledge, but he was now earning respect from his classmates who were in awe of his contributions during class discussions.

This renewed confidence was leading to a greater willingness for Billy to write about what he was reading, and his writing was descriptive, yet eloquent and succinctly answered the question. Billy was developing a knack for writing which caught the eye of the Head of School who felt Billy should write an article for the school magazine on the lessons we could learn from the current English novel in year 5. There is something to be said for passion, practice and confidence.

With just a few weeks remaining in term 3, Billy had progressed so much in literacy that the Head of Enrichment believed that Billy would benefit from some extension to further develop his thinking skills. However, Billy was still struggling with his maths, and he was finding it difficult to connect with specialist classes including art, french and physical education, which all caused him visible stress and anxiety. For Billy to be included in extension an Individual Program needed to be written to keep track of his goals, progress and outcomes in the areas of deficit for Billy. Kaufman (2018) highlights the importance of individual learning plans (ILP) for supporting the educational needs of twice-exceptional gifted students from a team approach perspective and to keep the parents fully informed.

Creating individual learning programs

It was wonderful to see Billy excelling and engaging with the subjects that involved reading and writing. He was performing extremely well in English, humanities and science/technology, and though maths was a battle, it was still front and centre each week and his teacher was proactive and highly supportive. So, these subjects were monitored for progress and an individual program with simple subject-by-subject goals was written for art, French and physical education, subjects for which Billy was way behind and highly challenged. Billy's goals for these subjects as set by him and learning support in consultation with the specialist teachers were as follows:

- **Art:** *Goal 1.* To listen to the teacher and have a go at the task according to what Billy believed he was meant to do from the teacher instructions. The teacher would write a numbered list of tasks on the board, and she would also check in on Billy regularly. Billy had been afraid of having a go in fear of making a mistake, which often left him behind by not working through the task. Perfectionism was also a very real challenge in Art, but Billy promised to always have a try. *Goal 2.* To work hard in class using all class time, and if he did, no homework would be set.

- **French:** *Goal 1.* To listen to the teacher during the teaching part of the lesson. *Goal 2.* To have a go at the oral part of French which would be part of each lesson. During the written activity, Billy would be excused. Instead, he could take his current reading book as long as he used this time to read. It was clear that Billy was not going to pursue French long-term, and written French caused him great stress and anxiety, hence he did just what was required to complete French oral assessments.

- **Physical education:** Physical education was another source of visible stress and anxiety for Billy. He was fine with individual sports, but he could not get his head around team sports, or how they worked. Team sports left him upset and vulnerable. *Goal 1.* Listen to the teacher, watch the skill demonstrations and participate in the skill parts of the lesson, including the drills and skill practice. *Goal 2.* During the team game practice assist the teacher and class by learning to score the game and scoring it for the class. You do not have to play the game. The teacher will help with this.

The goals for art, French and physical education were set up as an individual program for Billy and they were reviewed with his parents once a term, or more if needed, at which time his progress was reviewed, and his goals were adjusted as required.

It was agreed that extension classes for Billy would be done at lunch time or after school, or to coincide with English, a subject where Billy was excelling.

Extension and enrichment opportunities

His first extension activity came by way of special invitation to attend an animation workshop at the Australian Centre for the Moving Image, also known by the acronym ACMI (2019). This was a one-day event specifically designed for upper primary students that had a passion for animation or movie technology. The day required some preparation in the lead up. Billy had to write a 300-word narrative of his choice that could then be used to create an animation story. Billy had no trouble writing his narrative which he developed around a computer game that he hoped to create. He thought that the animation workshop might help him to create some colourful characters for his game bringing his game to life visually to support his future game development efforts.

Billy loved his day at ACMI where he created characters out of plasticine and a set from a cardboard box which he decorated to support his story. He learned to make his characters move by taking 30 photos per second of film with very minor adjustments being made to his plasticine figures every 10 photos. When the photos were merged and shown in a sequence they created a moving animation. To create his 30 second animation, he had to take 900 photos. He finished by layering a recorded narrative over the top of the animation. This day was enlightening for Billy where he learned enough by way of skills to continue with his own animation projects independently. He purchased a suitable camera and tripod and created sets and characters of his own out of plasticine or paper for future work. It is days like this that can start a movement for gifted students.

Again, the day at ACMI had boosted Billy's self-esteem. Not only was it a highly engaging day that aligned with his passions for creating something original using technology, but Billy had been acknowledged by his school for his unique skills. He had learned something new, and he was going to build on it.

In the proceeding weeks the Head of Enrichment invited Billy to join another group. Billy could just come to observe the group at first if he wished, but the Head of Enrichment believed that Billy had a lot to offer in this new challenge. The challenge was Da Vinci Decathlon (2019), a team competition comprising of eight team members covering ten different disciplines. A group of seven students were practicing at lunch time and they needed an 8th member. Billy entered the room and sat down as the group practiced an engineering problem. They had to make a bridge out of a set of materials provided that could span an imaginary waterway and hold a weight of 500 grams. The materials were light and sparse, and Billy wondered how the students would tackle the problem. Billy observed that first session and he was in awe of what the team produced. He decided he would like to join the group.

The students already knew Billy, and they were aware that he was a great thinker, but they also knew he had social challenges. To their credit they did not pressure him, they encouraged him to participate if he had a good idea and to just observe at other times. The 10 disciplines covered art and poetry, cartography (mapping skills), code breaking, creative producers (drama), an engineering challenge, an English challenge, general knowledge, a mathematical challenge, philosophy and science. Some of the disciplines didn't really suit Billy's skillset, but others were clear strengths. Billy's strengths were in the English challenge, philosophy, the engineering challenge and sometimes science. At times he was also able to contribute well to general knowledge and cartography.

The teacher encouraged the team to all work within their individual strengths, and to be involved and participate to the best of their ability in the other challenges. Even if this meant just listening or reading the problem, and more broadly encouraging the team. The teacher believed the students should lead in the challenges where their skills were high, but all needed to be attentive to each challenge, or their team would be penalised for disengagement or lack of focus.

Competition day came and Billy was excited to be a part of it. He had had six lunch time preparation sessions with the team, and he was ready to give his best effort, though he knew it would be hard to concentrate so well for 10 disciplines. Billy tried his best and he contributed well to the team. His input in his strength areas was exceptional because he looked at problems from very different and complex perspectives, but that was what this competition required. Outside the box thinking that was fresh and creative. His team was placed first in the English challenge, first in philosophy, second in the engineering challenge and third in general knowledge. They finished 5th overall from 39 competing teams. This had been the best result for the school that was still a relative newcomer to the Da Vinci Decathlon.

During the lunch time reflection which took place the day after the competition, the team highlighted Billy's efforts, particularly in English and philosophy. One girl stated, we simply wouldn't have won those sections without Billy's thinking which provided brilliant ideas for the broader group to build on. Ideas that eventually won the group those categories of Da Vinci. The girl went on to say that Billy's thinking was his superpower.

This again gave Billy social status and kudos in this group of gifted peers, and the news spread among the other students with a teacher on yard duty stating that while she had been on duty with Billy by her side, another student had congratulated him on his efforts in the Da Vinci Decathlon.

Social-emotional support and growth

There were still challenges at times. There were students who would intentionally bait or trigger Billy, and on occasions he didn't react well, once striking another student on the bus and chasing another student in rage at school after public ridicule. It was deemed important that we support Billy to understand himself better and to reduce his triggers. This led to support through a social skills group set up by the school counsellors. Baldwin et al. (2015) highlights the importance of providing social skills training for twice-exceptional students to enable them to understand their peers and themselves better, hence providing a smoother path in their interactions and personal growth. This Social Skills group resulted in Billy meeting other students very much like himself, and a friendship group quickly established.

This group went on to meet socially outside school, and with support from the counsellors the group also set up a board games gathering at school every Wednesday at lunch time in room 23. The group was advertised for any student in the school to attend, with Billy and his friends leading the session which included a welcome speech at the start with some participation etiquette expectations also shared to ensure the games session was conducted respectfully and appropriately.

Additionally, Billy met the same school counsellor every Tuesday morning, and at other times as needed along the way. The counseller made a point of mentoring Billy firstly to support his social and emotional needs, but secondly to support his learning and his talent in the academic fields where he was excelling. Informal goals were set to encourage Billy to try things outside his comfort zone in an effort to further extend his strengths. These goals were revisited, discussed and regularly adjusted through a clear mentoring process and they assisted in moving Billy's learning forward. Like in Smith (2024) the counsellor, as a teacher mentor was progressing Billy's achievement through the setting of goals and the transference of skills using a clear mentoring cycle.

Program success and sustainability

Billy was now excelling in English and humanities, and he was performing well in science/technology and steadily improving in maths. He had clear goals through an individual program that was supporting his difficulties in art, French and physical education. Billy was also being helped socially through his social skills group, and the mentor counsellor. Additionally his class teacher was assisting his organisation through the targeted use of his diary, with colour coding for each subject, and through further support with reminders shared through his timetable. Billy was establishing social cohorts through the social skills group but also through his highly able peers in extension sessions.

As everything started to align Billy was feeling that sense of belonging that only comes with knowing and understanding one's place. He was aware of his deficits and challenges, and the support measures in place, but he was largely being driven by his strengths which provided self-esteem and confidence. This self-esteem and confidence were enough to enable him to face his deficits, and as he faced them, they became less defining.

Sometimes it is not necessary to formally assess a student who might be twice exceptional. It is more important to get to know the student and develop a profile of their gifts and deficits. Then to develop an individualised approach that can work for the student to build their strengths and explicitly support their challenges and difficulties. What the students do by way of program needs to be fully communicated in school data bases and through relevant handover discussions for future teachers to view and build on. This is critical for ongoing support of such students. This is what had been done for Billy, and he was thriving in his new school after a slow start.

Experience tells me, the challenge is then to maintain this momentum year on year, because that is the key to supporting twice-exceptional students. When the right supports are in place such students will have enough confidence to keep trying, and with effort and practice supported by staff, parents and peers we so often see these students build routines for success and a learning scaffold that enables ongoing growth and progression.

Long-term outcomes

The educational road for twice-exceptional students is never perfect. There are regular bumps along the way, and new difficulties often arise, so supporting such students is always a work in progress. From the perspective of supporting educators, it is about being sensitive and responsive, considering the needs of the individual in each next step and providing appropriate and timely support. As students grow and develop it is critical to help them to understand themselves and others, to know their triggers and to manage them appropriately. With age and maturity, if students can self-regulate this will greatly enhance their progress. With ongoing support, the outcomes for twice-exceptional students are often very positive. Many will complete their final years of schooling, some with very good results, and many will be successful in their relationships and vocational endeavours. Some will find careers in areas that capture their gifts providing long-term reward and satisfaction, and many will lead very normal and successful lives throughout adulthood.

★ KEY TAKEAWAYS

- **Strengths-based approach:** Focusing on the strengths of twice-exceptional (2e) students, like Billy's passion for reading and abstract thinking, builds confidence and self-esteem. Leveraging strengths provides a foundation for addressing deficits, leading to both academic and social progress.

- **Individualised support plans:** Tailored Individual Learning Plans (ILPs) are essential for addressing the unique needs of 2e students. In Billy's case, subject-specific goals in art, French, and physical education helped him overcome stress and perfectionism while allowing him to shine in areas of strength.

- **The role of mentors and social skills training:** A dedicated mentor and participation in a Social Skills group supported Billy's social-emotional growth. Mentorship allowed for goal setting and self-reflection, while peer interactions within the group fostered friendships and reduced social isolation.

- **Extension opportunities to build confidence:** Providing opportunities such as the animation workshop and participation in the Da Vinci Decathlon allowed Billy to engage with his passions and demonstrate his exceptional abilities. These experiences reinforced his social connections and built his self-esteem.

- **Sustainable programming and collaboration:** Continuous review and communication among teachers, learning support staff, parents, and peers are critical for long-term success. Sustaining a system of targeted support ensures that the needs of 2e students, such as Billy, are met as they grow and transition through their schooling journey.

Chapter references

Australian Council for Educational Research (2019). *ACER General Ability Test*. ACER. General Ability Test.

Australian Centre for the Moving Image (2019). *Australian Centre for the Moving Image*. ACMI.

Baldwin, L., Omdal, S. N., & Pereles, D. (2015). Beyond stereotypes: Understanding, recognizing, and working with twice-exceptional learners. *Teaching Exceptional Children, 47*(4), 216–225.

Baum, S. M., Schader, R. M., & Owen, S. V. (2021). *To be gifted and learning disabled: Strength-based strategies for helping twice-exceptional students with LD, ADHD, ASD, and more*. Routledge.

Da Vinci Decathlon Excite Challenge Enrich (2019). *Da Vinci Decathlon*.

Kaufman, S. B. (Ed.). (2018). *Twice exceptional: Supporting and educating bright and creative students with learning difficulties*. Oxford University Press.

Reis, S. M., Baum, S. M., & Burke, E. (2014) An operational definition of twice-exceptional learners; Implications and applications, *Gifted Child Quarterly, 58*(3) 217–230.

Smith M. A. (2024), *Mentoring for Talent: A Practical Guide for Schools*. Amba Press.

Trail, B. A. (2022). *Twice-exceptional gifted children: Understanding, teaching, and counseling gifted students*. Routledge.

CHAPTER 10

Unravelling the '2e' Riddle: Quirky Homeschooling Adventures

Rhiannon Lowrey

The rise of homeschooling in Australia

In Victoria, the most recent figures show there were 11,912 homeschooled students as of December 2022, an increase of 36% since 2021 (Australian Bureau of Statistics, 2021). Across the country, I estimate, based on state and territory data, there are more than 43,000 legally registered homeschooled students. Estimation is required as there is no conclusive data collection at a national level. To date there is no indication as to why parents are opting to homeschool their children. In conversations with many homeschooling parents the common thread is that traditional schooling is not meeting the needs of their child. Homeschooling gives flexibility that many schools and traditional educational settings simply cannot accommodate.

Homeschooling has been seen as an alternative to traditional schooling due to it's highly flexible learning environment and its student centred and focused approach to learning. One reason for this is due to the adaptability of personalised learning plans. Personalised learning draws on insights from Kerr and Vuyk (2016). These plans can be adapted to traditional classroom settings by allowing for individualised goals and learning paths within the broader curriculum. Many schools are proficient in creating and writing personalised learning plans, these plans are usually crafted with specialised experts giving well intentioned and excellent strategies to supporting students with additional learning needs, both in a support capacity and an extension context.

Challenges in traditional school settings

A major conflict is the way in which schools communicate what the individual needs of students are to teachers, especially in a secondary context. As there are many teachers interacting daily with students, the students' needs are usually kept in a centralised database and there is not always the quick and simple summary of needs that teachers might require quickly.

A second conflict is when the plan is written specifically for the individual student as per the intention, schools do not provide clear context that there is more than one student present in the class. In a class of 26 students there could be a minimum of 3-4 students who have complex needs including a need for extension. Unfortunately, many teachers prioritise those students who require support in order to achieve standard. This means that much of the teacher's attention is split between students who require assistance to begin a task, and those that require behaviour management issues. This does not leave much time for supporting students who are more than capable of the standard to be extended and challenged.

Another conflict in Australian schools was the implementation of the Nationally Consistent Collection of Data (NCCD). The NCCD based upon the 1992 Disability Discrimination Act and the 2005 Disability Standards for Schools, introduced an equity system of education for students in learning communities with disabilities. Being gifted with a learning challenge, although in many ways similar to having a learning difficulty is not considered a disability, thus eliminating these students from gaining access to supports and funding. The model of funding support in education is a 3-tiered approach that offers more funding for students requiring higher levels of support for a diagnosed disability.

Gifted students are mentioned in the NCCD documents, they are required to gain support under the lowest level identified as quality differentiated teaching practices (QDTP). This ultimately means that teachers are not offered any time or support to create programs that work for these learners as the priority is provided to supporting the needs of students with higher funding levels.

This might seem like a pessimistic approach to the support structure in schools. Many educational institutions have support teams of 10-15 people to help 'supported' students as they can number 30-40% of the classroom. Some schools have 1 staff member who supports extension programs or gifted education programs. In 2024 all schools in New South Wales are required to have a 'gifted' program to assist gifted learners with their personal growth.

Many parents have become frustrated with the idea that their child cannot see twelve months growth in twelve months of schooling. Their child might have been well ahead of the cohort before the year commenced but due to a lack of support they resort to homeschooling to avoid their child from falling into invisibility, depression or even school refusal.

Learning approaches and curriculum flexibility

There has been much debate over the best kind of learning in Australian schools, the debate continues to rage over VCE, VM (Vocational Major), VCE hybrid, IB (International Baccalaureate), inquiry based learning, project based learning, concept based learning, ROTE learning. Jolly and Matthews (2017) emphasise the benefits of flexibility in teaching methods and curriculum delivery for gifted students. I would argue that the model that underpins the school curriculum is arbitrary. Many homeschooled students are able to pick from writing an essay, to painting a picture, to constructing a scientific experiment and report, on whatever big idea or area of interest they have at the time. This capacity to demonstrate their knowledge in a way that is organic and natural is much more in line with the greater community outside of school.

If students require flexibility to feel comfortable, then they also require minor discomfort to create endurance and resilience. I often say in the context of my classroom, it is okay to sit in discomfort, that means you are becoming more flexible. Discomfort does not and should not hurt, but it can challenge. The idea that students should only present knowledge in a singular way, or their preferred learning style does not help the learner to grow in areas of weakness. This is why a mixed approach is preferred for gifted learners where they can, complete the classwork, demonstrate capacity and grow in areas requiring growth. Not all areas will be perfect. This is when a students should use the knowledge to make something new or present this information in a way that makes sense to the knowledge, not just to the subject or teacher.

Exploring how educators can incorporate flexible learning opportunities, such as project-based learning and independent study projects, into traditional classroom environments is valuable. Australian researchers, Jarvis and Henderson (2019), delve into the advantages of acceleration and enrichment programs for gifted students. Offering practical advice on how schools can implement these strategies, including subject acceleration, grade skipping, and the provision of extracurricular enrichment activities.

Extension and enrichment programs are valuable when facilitated by someone who is passionate and an open thinker. Unfortunately I have seen in both school and home school settings, the purchase of mathematics textbooks at a higher level than the chronological age of the child. Using these the child is able to read and compute skills at a higher and higher level. As a secondary teacher in the area of maths, I am often advised that these students are gifted. It is true that they are very good mathematicians, but I find they can only repeat the knowledge in the same way and format as they have learned it. Progression of skills through more senior textbooks in maths and science is not an indication of giftedness in that subject – the skills that are being displayed are application of formula, memory and interest, rather than applicable intelligence. For example, when teaching 'advanced mathematics' I found many of my students struggled with a measurement task deeply founded in number and algebra skills. For a mathematics assessment in measurement, I gave each student a blank piece of grid paper and a paper cup. The assessment task was to 'tell me everything you can about this cup'. We had studied the typical topics, surface area, volume, capacity etc, and yet many students failed to be able to tell me much more than the dimensions of the cup. Many were unable to identify the name as a frustrum, as a cup is part of a cone, a concept covered in class. This reinforces that progression is about the application of the next formula, the understanding and most interesting part of mathematics is when the knowledge you have sparked creates more questions including why, how, where is this related etc.

Beyond academic achievement: Social-emotional considerations

Another huge factor for many students transitioning from traditional education to homeschooling is recognising the social and emotional challenges faced by many gifted students. Gross (2017) discusses the importance of providing comprehensive support which provides strategies for educators to create a classroom culture that addresses the unique social and emotional needs of gifted students. Many students are given the label of being gifted, without formal diagnosis. This could be based on parent observations over time in which they identified that their child has been able to acquire knowledge and skills at an early age or met proficiency quickly. Without discrimination, these children and learners are often very capable and excellent learners. The gifted students who need more support in the classroom are often the ones that have had a formal diagnosis and have had external and internal pressure placed on them due to experts, medical professional observations, and opinions.

Gifted students are often much harder on themselves, than their age equivalent peers (Dixon et al., 2020; Flett et al., 2019). Many psychologists such as Attwood (2018) and Gross (2017) agree that perfectionism and depression are more prevalent within the gifted community than in many others. Neurodiverse people such as boys with an autism diagnosis, often do not exhibit any care to fit social norms. They are happy with who they are and people accept that about them. Females with an autism diagnosis tend to be more in tune to the social norms around them and they expend a great deal of effort 'fitting in'. Many prepubescent and pubescent girls struggle with identity and fitting in, but they have the capacity to be able to decipher and understand many social norms and unwritten rules around how to be successful in interactions. Females with autism are known to mask more and have more outbursts in private after a large socially taxing event like school (de Houting, 2020).

Inspired by the work of Townsend and Plunkett (2016), collaborative learning can be particularly beneficial for gifted students. It enables ways for them to facilitate meaningful group work and peer interactions within the classroom enhancing learning and social development. This is inconsistent with homeschooling on a day-to-day basis. Home schoolers are able to meet together in libraries and homes across the country, however these need to be organised and facilitated in a structured way. It is easier for collaboration in school settings, however the groups for collaboration need to be carefully constructed.

Alternative education models and future directions

There are many models of school that can be taught at home such as Euka, Pangea (Haileybury model), Dwight school, Charlotte Mason, and distance education. These organisations are ready to support 2e learners at home with a robust curriculum. They are all listed on the Home Education Australia website, outlining the benefits for each model, leaving it up to parents to decide which is the best one for their family and learner.

The obstacle for traditional schooling institutions is where to operate. Most schools have a foundation and underlying idea of how schools should look and operate. Montessori is different to Steiner, as is VCE and IB. Finding the right school and the right curriculum is hard. The pedagogy of how to learn is often written in the fabric of the school. Many traditional schools get excellent VCE and academic results, offering a more traditional way of learning, focusing on skill acquisition, memorisation and recall of facts. Learners who don't experience any difficulties often thrive in this environment, yet those with working memory issues and processing speed issues, do not and soon they begin to disengage. I recently conducted a survey with university students. I found that although they achieved success in this traditional model, they found it was not inclusive, rather it was results driven and the teacher did not always know the learner. In contrast those students who learnt under a more modern, inquiry based approach, said that school was engaging, relationships and discussions with teachers was rich and robust, but they said it did not really prepare students for the real world. They felt like their voices were valid at school but outside school they were unfamiliar with the model or the learning style.

There is only a handful of Australian schools that have successfully integrated homeschooling approaches into their programs for gifted students and these are usually subject based rather than whole school modelled. In 2023 the winners of innovative education were Larrakeyah Primary School, Westbourne Grammar School, Ravenswood School for Girls, Balcombe Grammar School, Mancel College, Matthew Flinders Anglican College, Ormiston College, and Pulteney Grammar School. The schools showcase the innovative ways in which educators can support gifted learners by adopting a more personalised, flexible, and supportive approach to education. Proactive schools are out there and often they are independent or private schools rather than public at a secondary level. This is due to community buy in and Boards willing to risk changing education to see great reward.

This chapter concludes by emphasising the potential of homeschooling strategies for transforming the educational experiences of gifted students in traditional settings. It calls for educators to see, acknowledge, accept, and embrace these approaches, adapting them to the unique contexts of their schools and classrooms. It calls for educators to better meet the needs of gifted learners, after embracing 2e learners and differentiated learning pedagogy. It is not just about differentiating approaches, to the same concepts in the hope that educators will find that they are meeting the needs of students at all levels in a more meaningful way.

⭐ KEY TAKEAWAYS

- **The flexibility of homeschooling:** Homeschooling offers a highly adaptable and student-centred learning environment, which is often more conducive to the unique needs of gifted and twice-exceptional (2e) students. Personalised learning plans allow for individualised goals and learning paths that are difficult to achieve in traditional classrooms.

- **Challenges in traditional schooling:** Traditional schooling often struggles to meet the needs of gifted students due to limited resources, competing priorities for teacher attention, and a lack of formal support or funding for gifted education under frameworks like the Nationally Consistent Collection of Data (NCCD).

- **Importance of emotional and social support:** Gifted students often experience heightened emotional and social challenges, including perfectionism, depression, and difficulty fitting into social norms, particularly among neurodiverse learners. Addressing these needs through tailored support is critical for their wellbeing and success.

- **Integrating homeschooling strategies into schools:** Schools can learn from homeschooling models by incorporating flexibility, project-based learning, and independent study into their programs. Strategies such as acceleration, enrichment programs, and collaborative learning can better support gifted learners within a traditional setting.

- **Innovative and personalised approaches:** A few Australian schools have successfully implemented personalised and innovative approaches to education, showcasing the potential for hybrid models that blend the benefits of homeschooling with traditional school environments. Embracing these strategies can transform the educational experiences of gifted students.

Chapter references

Australian Bureau of Statistics. (2021). *School enrolments and homeschooling data*.
Attwood, T. (2018). *The complete guide to Asperger's syndrome*. Jessica Kingsley Publishers.
Dixon, F. A., Moon, S. M., & Towner, J. C. (2020). *The Handbook of Secondary Gifted Education*. Routledge.
de Houting, J. (2020). Neurodiversity and the double empathy problem. *Autism, 24*(6), 1591–1594.
Flett, G. L., Hewitt, P. L., Nepon, T., & Besser, A. (2019). Perfectionism and academic difficulties in gifted students: A systematic review. *Gifted Child Quarterly, 63*(2), 118-134.
Gross, M. U. M. (2017). *Exceptionally gifted children* (2nd ed.). Routledge.
Jarvis, J., & Henderson, L. (2019). The benefits of acceleration and enrichment programs for gifted learners. *Australian Journal of Gifted Education, 28*(2), 17-28.
Jolly, J. L., & Matthews, M. S. (2017). *Beyond gifted education: Designing and implementing advanced academic programs*. Prufrock Press.
Kerr, B., & Vuyk, M. A. (2016). Giftedness and learning disabilities: A study of twice-exceptional learners. *Journal for the Education of the Gifted, 39*(4), 319-327.
Townsend, M. A., & Plunkett, M. (2016). Collaborative learning and social interaction for gifted students. *Gifted Child Quarterly, 60*(3), 165-177.
Nationally Consistent Collection of Data (NCCD). (2023). *Guidelines and implementation in Australian schools*. Australian Government.

CHAPTER II
Celebrating 2e Success Stories: Role Models to Roll After

Rhiannon Lowrey

Celebrating neurodiversity

Celebrating neurodiversity is crucial for several reasons:

- **Inclusivity and acceptance:** When we celebrate neurodiversity, we create a culture of inclusivity and acceptance. People with neurodiverse conditions, such as autism, ADHD, or dyslexia, often face stigma and discrimination. By celebrating their unique strengths and perspectives, we foster a sense of belonging and reduce the negative impact of societal biases.
- **Unlocking hidden potential:** Neurodiversity brings a wide range of talents and abilities. Many neurodiverse individuals excel in fields like mathematics, technology, art, and innovation. By celebrating neurodiversity, we harness this untapped potential and provide opportunities for individuals to thrive and contribute meaningfully to society.
- **Promoting innovation:** Neurodiverse individuals often possess unconventional thinking and problem-solving skills. Celebrating neurodiversity encourages diverse thought processes and can lead to innovative solutions in various domains, including science, business, and technology.

- **Enhancing empathy and understanding:** When we celebrate neurodiversity, it helps neurotypical individuals better understand and empathise with neurodiverse individuals. This increased understanding can lead to more inclusive workplaces, schools, and communities.
- **Mental health and wellbeing:** Celebrating neurodiversity can reduce the mental health challenges often faced by neurodiverse individuals due to societal pressures to conform. It promotes self-acceptance, self-esteem, and overall mental wellbeing.
- **Legislation and policy changes:** Celebrating neurodiversity can drive changes in legislation and policies to ensure equal rights, accommodations, and opportunities for neurodiverse individuals. It can lead to more inclusive educational practices, workplace policies, and healthcare services.

Celebrating neurodiversity goes beyond mere discourse; it is an active commitment to recognising and valuing the unique abilities and perspectives of all individuals. By doing so, we can create a more inclusive, innovative, and empathetic society that benefits everyone, regardless of their neurodiverse characteristics.

Unveiling the heroes within

Sharing the success stories of those who have gone before can invigorate resilience in 2e learners, when facing challenges in school and beyond.

Albert Einstein: The renowned physicist Albert Einstein is often cited as a potential example of a 2e individual. He exhibited exceptional mathematical and scientific talents but faced difficulties in traditional education settings and language development during his early years.

Thomas Edison: The prolific inventor Thomas Edison, known for his contributions to the light bulb and phonograph, struggled with formal education due to learning challenges. He is another historical figure speculated to be twice exceptional.

**Temple Grandin:** Dr Temple Grandin, an autism advocate and expert in animal science, is considered twice exceptional. She has autism and faces social and sensory challenges but also possesses an extraordinary ability to understand animal behaviour and design livestock handling systems.

Richard Branson: Business magnate and founder of the Virgin Group, Richard Branson struggled with dyslexia in his childhood. Despite his reading challenges, he became a successful entrepreneur, highlighting his exceptional creativity and leadership skills.

**Steven Spielberg:** The renowned filmmaker Steven Spielberg faced learning difficulties, particularly in reading, during his early years. Despite these challenges, he went on to become one of the most celebrated directors in the history of cinema.

Agatha Christie: The famous mystery novelist Agatha Christie is believed to have struggled with dysgraphia, which made writing challenging. Despite this, she authored numerous best-selling novels, showcasing her exceptional storytelling and deductive skills.

**John Nash:** The Nobel laureate mathematician John Nash, portrayed in the movie "A Beautiful Mind", had a brilliant mathematical brain yet struggled with schizophrenia, highlighting the complexity of being twice exceptional.

Stephen Hawking: The world-renowned theoretical physicist Stephen Hawking had amyotrophic lateral sclerosis (ALS), a neurodegenerative disease. Despite his physical limitations, he made significant contributions to the field of theoretical physics and cosmology.

 **Helen Keller:** Helen Keller was both deaf and blind due to an illness in her infancy. She became an author, political activist, and lecturer, inspiring countless people with her determination and advocacy for the disabled.

James Durbin: Diagnosed with both Asperger's syndrome and Tourette syndrome, James Durbin was a finalist on American Idol and has pursued a successful music career.

 **Daryl Hannah:** Actress Daryl Hannah has autism, a condition she has spoken openly about. She has had a successful acting career, starring in films like "Splash" and "Kill Bill".

Dan Aykroyd: Comedian and actor Dan Aykroyd was diagnosed with Tourette syndrome and Asperger's syndrome. He co-wrote and starred in the classic film "Ghostbusters".

 **Michael Phelps:** Olympic swimmer Michael Phelps, who holds numerous records, has spoken about his ADHD diagnosis and the challenges he faced in managing his energy and focus.

Justin Timberlake: Pop star Justin Timberlake has openly discussed his struggle with obsessive-compulsive disorder (OCD) and attention deficit hyperactivity disorder (ADHD). This has not prevented him from being a successful musician and film star.

From struggles to superpowers

Every 2e (twice-exceptional) student embarks on a unique educational journey, facing both extraordinary abilities and distinct challenges. These remarkable individuals are often overlooked, misunderstood, or underestimated due to the complexities of their neurodiversity. However, the stories of their resilience, self-discovery, and unwavering determination serve as powerful beacons of hope and inspiration. In this exploration, we'll celebrate the heroes of neurodiversity, prioritising those from Melbourne and across Australia, by sharing their remarkable journeys, highlighting their achievements, and emphasising the importance of recognising and supporting the potential of every 2e learner.

Navigating the complexities

Meet Sarah, a Melbourne-based student who discovered her 2e identity in high school. Despite exhibiting a high level of creativity and passion for the arts, she struggled with dyslexia and ADHD. Sarah's journey was marked by feelings of frustration and inadequacy as she faced academic challenges that didn't reflect her true potential. With the support of her parents, teachers, and a neuropsychological evaluation, she received a tailored education plan that recognised her strengths and provided accommodations for her weaknesses. Sarah's story illustrates the importance of early identification and support for 2e students, allowing them to flourish academically and artistically.

The power of perseverance

In Sydney, James, a 2e student with autism, embarked on his educational journey determined to break stereotypes. He faced scepticism from educators who doubted his ability to excel academically. However, James channelled his intense focus and passion for mathematics into winning a national mathematics competition. His achievement not only shattered stereotypes but also inspired educators to recognise the untapped potential of 2e students with autism. James's story underscores the importance of embracing neurodiversity and providing opportunities for 2e students to showcase their unique talents.

A beacon of hope

In Brisbane, Emily, a 2e student with sensory processing differences, encountered challenges in social interactions and sensory overload in traditional classroom settings. However, her school recognised the importance of creating an inclusive environment. They implemented sensory-friendly classrooms, social skills programs, and peer mentorship initiatives. With these supports, Emily not only improved her social interactions but also became a source of inspiration for her peers. Her story demonstrates the transformative impact of fostering inclusivity and providing tailored support to 2e students, enabling them to thrive and find a sense of belonging.

A vision for the future

Back in Melbourne, Liam, a 2e student with a passion for robotics, faced scepticism about his ability to excel in STEM (Science, Technology, Engineering, and Mathematics) fields due to his ADHD and dysgraphia. However, Liam's determination and supportive parents led him to participate in robotics competitions. He not only excelled but also won international acclaim for his innovative projects. Liam's journey exemplifies the importance of breaking barriers and providing opportunities for 2e students to pursue their passions, regardless of stereotypes or initial doubts.

A voice for change

In Adelaide, Grace, a 2e student with ADHD and anxiety, decided to become an advocate for neurodiversity awareness. Her personal journey of self-acceptance and understanding inspired her to raise awareness about 2e students' unique needs. Grace organised workshops, seminars, and awareness campaigns in her school and community. Her efforts not only educated others about neurodiversity but also created a supportive network for 2e students. Grace's story highlights the power of self-advocacy and the role 2e students can play in fostering understanding and acceptance.

A teacher's influence

In Perth, Matthew, a 2e student with dyslexia and giftedness, experienced the transformative impact of a supportive teacher. His primary school teacher recognised his potential and provided personalised instruction. This support allowed Matthew to develop his reading skills and tap into his giftedness. Matthew's story emphasises the crucial role educators play in identifying and nurturing the potential of 2e students. It also highlights the importance of professional development for teachers to better support neurodiverse learners.

***

These stories from Melbourne, Sydney, Brisbane, Adelaide, Perth, and across Australia demonstrate that every 2e student is a hero on their own unique journey. By recognising their strengths, understanding their challenges, and providing tailored support, we can unleash the full potential of 2e learners. These heroes inspire us to celebrate neurodiversity, break stereotypes, and create inclusive educational environments that empower every 2e student to thrive. Through their stories, we learn that with the right support and mindset, neurodiversity can be a source of strength and innovation, enriching the educational landscape for all.

Teachers as shapers of destiny

Behind every success story is an educator who believed in the potential of a 2e student and provided the support needed to nurture that potential. These remarkable teachers recognised that every child is unique and capable of extraordinary achievements, even when faced with learning challenges or disabilities. They not only identified the hidden talents and strengths of their students but also championed their causes, helping them break through barriers and reach their full potential. Here, we'll spotlight the stories of such champion educators who have made a profound impact on the lives of 2e students.

Dr Linda Silverman

Achievement: Dr Linda Silverman is a renowned educational psychologist and the founder of the Gifted Development Centre. She has dedicated her life to understanding and advocating for the needs of gifted and 2e individuals.

Contribution: Dr Silverman's work involves identifying giftedness and learning disabilities in students. Her research and assessments have helped countless 2e children receive the appropriate support and accommodations they need to excel academically.

Penina Kiss

Achievement: Penina Kiss a catholic education teacher and gifted specialist has received national recognition for her work with students, revolutionising the way that students are being taught in the NSW regional Diocese.

Contribution: Penina transformed her classroom into an inclusive and supportive environment where 2e students could thrive. Her dedication to understanding the unique needs of each student, along with her creative teaching methods, has been instrumental in their success. She emphasises the importance of celebrating neurodiversity and focusing on strengths. Penina's Learning Model for Gifted Education provides a comprehensive framework for identifying, supporting, and nurturing the potential of gifted and 2e students. Her work recognises the importance of individualised and challenging instruction, social-emotional support, and collaboration among all stakeholders to create a successful educational experience for gifted learners.

Chris Ulmer

Achievement: Chris Ulmer is a former special education teacher who gained fame for his "Special Books by Special Children" project.

Contribution: Chris travels the world interviewing individuals with various disabilities, including 2e students. His compassionate approach aims to break down stereotypes and promote inclusion. He showcases the incredible talents and stories of 2e individuals, challenging society's perceptions and inspiring acceptance.

Esther Wojcicki

Achievement: Esther Wojcicki is an esteemed educator, journalist, and author who has received numerous awards for her contributions to education. Her book how to raise successful people is a brilliant example of the power of parents and educators working together to see strength, and beauty in all abilities.

Contribution: She highlights the importance of trust, autonomy, and respect in the classroom. Her innovative teaching methods and dedication to fostering creativity have allowed 2e students to flourish academically and artistically. Esther advocates for a growth mindset and believes that all students have the potential to excel.

*　*　*

The common thread among these educators is their unwavering belief in the potential of 2e students and their dedication to providing the support needed to nurture that potential. They prioritise understanding each student's unique strengths and challenges and tailor their teaching approaches accordingly. Whether through groundbreaking research, inclusive classroom environments, or innovative teaching methods, these educators champion neurodiversity and celebrate the strengths of every child. Their commitment to fostering a growth mindset and promoting inclusion serves as a testament to the transformative power of teachers in shaping the destinies of 2e students.

Families as anchors of support

In these stories, families stand as steadfast pillars of support, offering unwavering love, encouragement, and advocacy. Here we will share how families collaborated with educators to create an environment that allowed their 2e children to shine, demonstrating the profound impact of familial support.

Families play a crucial role in supporting their 2e children. Here are some practical ways in which families can help their 2e children, along with real-life resources and links for further information:

- **Understand their needs:** Learn about twice-exceptionality and your child's specific strengths and challenges. Understanding their unique profile is the first step in providing appropriate support.
- **Advocate for accommodations:** Work with your child's school to ensure they receive appropriate accommodations and support. This may include an Individualised Education Plan (IEP).
- **Seek out specialists:** Consult with professionals who specialise in twice-exceptionality, such as psychologists, therapists, or educational consultants.

- **Build a supportive environment:** Create a nurturing and understanding home environment where your child feels safe to express their thoughts and emotions.
- **Encourage their interests:** Support your child's passions and interests, even if they are unconventional. These interests can be a source of motivation and self-esteem.
- **Teach self-advocacy:** Help your child develop self-advocacy skills, teaching them to communicate their needs and preferences to teachers and peers.
- **Balance challenge and support:** Find a balance between challenging your child to reach their potential and providing emotional and academic support.
- **Connect with other parents:** Join local or online support groups for parents of 2e children to share experiences and resources.
- **Explore online resources:** Utilise online platforms, websites, and forums dedicated to twice-exceptionality for information and guidance.
- **Celebrate achievements:** Recognise and celebrate your child's accomplishments, no matter how small. Positive reinforcement can boost their confidence.
- **Model perseverance:** Demonstrate resilience and perseverance in your own life to set an example for your child.
- **Promote a growth mindset:** Encourage your child to adopt a growth mindset, emphasising that effort and learning from mistakes lead to growth and success.

Remember that every 2e child is unique, and what works best for one may not work for another. Tailor your support to your child's specific strengths and challenges and seek professional guidance when needed.

 **KEY TAKEAWAYS**

- **The value of celebrating neurodiversity:** Recognising and celebrating neurodiversity fosters inclusivity, reduces stigma, and enhances empathy, understanding, and innovation. This shift from tolerance to celebration highlights the potential of neurodiverse individuals.

- **The power of role models and success stories:** Historical and contemporary examples of successful 2e individuals demonstrate that neurodiversity can be a strength rather than a limitation. These stories inspire hope and provide practical examples of how challenges can be transformed into unique abilities.

- **The importance of support systems:** The success of 2e individuals relies heavily on a network of support, including dedicated educators, understanding families, and appropriate resources. When these systems work together effectively, they create an environment where 2e individuals can thrive and reach their full potential.

CHAPTER 12
Resources for 2e Success
Dr Susan Nikakis

This chapter has lists, checklist, plays, books, websites, Strategies for Emotional Regulations, Tools for Collecting Information on Strengths, Interests, Learning Styles, Instruments Helpful in Identification of ADHD, SPD, Attention Deficit Hyperactivity Disorder (ADHD), Diagnostic Criteria and Characteristics, and more! Basically, tools of the trade and other resources to help teachers identify and cater for 2e students

Neurodiversity is the word of the moment

The movement is really accelerating now. We are truly on the cusp of societal change. The number of online conferences, podcasts, webinars, and Facebook groups focusing on twice exceptionality has grown exponentially in the past three years.

There are plays about 2e individuals (*The Curious Incident of the Dog in the Night* and *Dear Evan Hansen*), and portrayals of 2e people in TV shows (*The Good Doctor*, *The Big Bang Theory*, and *Silicon Valley*).

I think one reason we've come so far is because we're fascinated by the stories of innovators in technology like Steve Jobs, Mark Zuckerberg and Bill Gates who seem to be twice exceptional, or at a minimum are very quirky. People are beginning to realise that innovators are out-of-the-box thinkers who may well be neurodiverse, differently wired, or bright and quirky. As teachers we must advocate for twice-exceptional students to have their asynchronous needs catered for at school.

Quick tips for teachers

- **Educate yourself.** In addition to learning about twice-exceptionality, you may want to learn more about giftedness and your student's diagnoses. You may also want to learn more about your school policies, your state's laws and federal laws.
- **Assemble a team.** When thinking through how to productively intervene and advocate on behalf of your student it can be helpful to identify potential allies and to build a support network.
- **Evaluate the environments that your student is a part of.** Consider how extracurricular programs, social spaces and other school provisions are already working for your student in the educational setting.
- **Set goals.** Once you've educated yourself, assemble a team and evaluate your student's situation. You will then be ready to set goals based on the information, people and resources you have.
- **Monitor and modify.** As you implement your plans for your student observe how these changes are affecting them. Remember that changes can often take many weeks to take hold and produce the outcomes you were hoping for.
- **The resources**. Include physical, psychological, academic, and medical, not to mention the personnel involved. All directly affect the multi-exceptional child's academic achievement as much as the child's own capacity and disability.
- **Teacher and school attitudes** about the twice-exceptional child and the child's abilities and disabilities contribute directly to the child's adjustment to school and their talent development progress.

What educators can do

Prioritise student choice: 2e students often have a much more difficult time focusing on topics and tasks that don't interest them. When they're provided with opportunities to study topics for which they are naturally curious – or to show their knowledge in ways that they find interesting – these students are much more likely to fully engage.

Strive for a 4:1 ratio of praise to redirection: Because of their area(s) of disability, 2e students are often quite accustomed to criticism from adults. Not only that, but these students are usually well aware of their deficiencies and extremely frustrated with themselves for not being able to measure up. A 4:1 ratio of genuine praise to direction can help build much-needed confidence in 2e students while also showing them they are worthy of praise.

Build movement breaks into the school day: In many schools, students don't have enough opportunities to move around, and 2e students require movement breaks in order to re-centre themselves, relieve stress, and improve focus. Depending on the grade level, movement breaks will look different in terms of type and frequency, but the important part is making sure they are built into each school day.

Differentiate as often as possible: 2e students have both exceptional strengths and exceptional challenges (a combination often described as "asynchronous development"). There's a pronounced discrepancy between their strengths and their weaknesses, as well as between their abilities and what they achieve. When educators truly differentiate their instruction, they help 2e students build on strengths and develop areas of weakness so that the gap between their abilities and achievement is reduced.

Explicitly teach SEL skills: Social and emotional learning is a high priority for 2e students because it's an area that's often challenging for them. The more that educators explicitly teach 2e students a vocabulary for their emotions and practical ways to self-regulate, the better able 2e students are to understand, and eventually control, their intense emotions. When 2e students are better able to control their emotions, they (SEL) are more able able to fully participate at school.

Build perseverance: Because of their giftedness, 2e students aren't usually pushed to the edge of their understanding. So, when they do find themselves at the edge, they become anxious. Explicitly teaching a growth mindset helps 2e students understand that new skills can be developed over time. Praising even the smallest of successes during the learning process can make a big impact for these students over time.

Each of these pedagogical approaches is usually considered a hallmark of good teaching. But the important distinction here is that for 2e students, these approaches are not just helpful – they're essential. When we create school communities that accommodate 2e students, we help them become the best versions of themselves and that's a gift that will keep on giving.

School accommodations and modifications

2e accommodations may be as informal as providing notes prior to class or permitting doodling or fidgeting to help with focus. Accommodations ultimately come down to knowing how the child's condition manifests, and valuing strengths and interests over weaknesses.

Some ideas for 2e classroom accommodations include:

- Extended time on assessments and assignments (ask for Measures of Academic Progress tests, which are not timed).
- Individualised curriculums, created through diagnostic assessments that test their knowledge before and after learning units.
- Alternative projects, especially if the child can explore concepts through their interests.
- Assistive technologies (using recording devices, typing rather than writing, learning apps, etc.).
- Multimedia resources (such as video lessons over typical lectures). Use of thematic instruction that can include the child's passions or interests.

Difficulty	Keys
Focusing and sustaining attention	• Employ environmental modifications • Use alternate entry points aligned to students' strengths and interests • Use technology • Try a novelty • Allow attention sustainers: permitting gum chewing, listening to music using headphones, underlining, or highlighting text when reading, doodling, or playing with clay or silly putty while listening can all help
Acquiring information with limited reading skills	• Use a multiple intelligence approach • Reverse the usual sequence, i.e., begin with experience • Teach through projects • Teach through the arts (dramas, visual arts, poetry, etc.) • Use seminar instruction, lively discussion groups, simulations, and moral dilemmas • Use primary sources such as interviews, guest speakers, demonstrations • Engage students in discussion using supporting text • Take advantage of multimedia presentations • Use picture books
Organising information	• Employ teaching materials with a visual component • Provide books on tape • Use text-to-speech software • Use advance organisers • Provided skeletal outlines • Use visual models and recipes

Difficulty	Keys
Remembering details and noncontextually materials	- Teach and model webbing, storyboarding, using flowcharts
- Provide software programs that help with writing and organising
- Use inductive teaching strategies
- Provide meaningful contexts for integrating facts and strategies
- Use mnemonic devices
- Use, and teach how to use, visual imagery
- Allow students to use highlighter pens to mark important concepts (if rules permit it)
- Encourage students to teach each other
- Use a word processor or laptop computer for notetaking
- Provide students with a copy of the information that highlights the key facts
- Have students sequence activities after a lesson or event
- Have students tape directions or information
- Provide students with environmental cues and prompts (posted rules, steps for performing tasks, etc.)

Difficulty	Keys
Written expression (these suggestions assume that writing does not equate to paper-and-pencil tasks. When possible, students should complete writing tasks using a word processor)	• Allow students to use resources in the environment to recall information (notes, textbooks, pictures, etc.) • Have students outline, summarise, or underline information to be remembered • Tell students what to listen for when being given directions or receiving information • Have students immediately repeat or paraphrase directions or information • Use artistic (visual and performing) scientific, and technological products to communicate knowledge • Use portfolio assessment of products and performances in addition to grading written products • Use technology (e.g., word processing programs with spelling and grammar checks, electronic speller, word predictive software or organisational software) • Establish writing routines through ongoing discussion and practice • Extend the time for completing written assignments or tests • Instruct students about using graphic organisers • Provide clear written expectations for writing tasks (rubrics) • Encourage students to proofread for only one type of error at a time

Assistive technology

Think about the burgeoning field of Artificial Intelligence (AI)! As a baby boomer I started life in Sydney, Australia with a small fat black and white television. Now look!

I think one reason we've come so far is because we're fascinated by the stories of innovators in technology like Steve Jobs, Mark Zuckerberg and Bill Gates who seem to be twice exceptional, or at a minimum appear to be very quirky. People are beginning to realise that innovators are out-of-the-box thinkers who may well be neurodiverse, differently wired, or bright and quirky. As teachers we must advocate for twice-exceptional students to have their asynchronous needs catered for at school.

For quite a while, assistive technology has given twice-exceptional students multiple ways to support their executive functioning skills and to demonstrate knowledge. It has allowed them to move from dependence to independence. However, the use of artificial intelligence such as ChatGPT raises concerns.

As a teacher, I learned and practiced differentiation, identifying student strengths, needs, interests, and talents, and making appropriate adaptations and accommodations. According to Carol Ann Tomlinson, differentiation is accomplished in three areas: *Content*, information about a topic; *Process*, activities to achieve a result; and *Product*, what is produced. Maker also includes *Environment*.

Jade Bowler says AI limitations including bias, a lack of real-world understanding, emotional intelligence, an inability to verify information (sources), and an inability for critical thinking is a concern with AI technolgies. Bowler offers the following strategies for using ChatGPT. Use it:

- As a summary tool
- For role-play
- To generate flashcards
- To critique an essay
- For creative writing prompts
- For questions in the Socratic Method (I adore the Socratic method)
- To grade homework
- As a brainstorming partner

What else could teachers working with 2e students do to effectively use ChatGPT and AI as we move forward? The following action steps for educators and students may be helpful:

For teachers:

- Use reliable sources, acquire knowledge and understanding about AI
- Learn the advantages and limitations of AI
- Analyse your current use of differentiation within *Content*, *Process*, *Product* and *Environment*

- Provide instruction to students about the advantages and limitations of AI
- Analyse similarities and differences between AI and the human brain
- Provide students with expectations/rubrics and guided practice for using AI
- Stay current with the newest information
- Make adaptations in curriculum as needed

For students:

- Use reliable sources, acquire knowledge and understanding about AI
- Learn the advantages and limitations of AI and the human brain
- Analyse similarities and differences between AI and the human brain
- Recognise that human creativity and innovation are an integral part of the process
- Synthesise information about how AI can be applied to schoolwork and beyond
- Apply AI as a tool to enhance your creations
- Experiment creating products using a combination of AI and the human brain

The more we know and understand, the more we can analyse using technology and apply new information and the better we will become at synthesising the information into new and exciting products. Even as we interact with the newest – and sometimes scariest – technology, we can help 2e students enjoy the process and experience "aha moments."

In the classroom

Successful programs for gifted students with a learning disability are programs that recognise their giftedness and provide educational opportunities that allow for enrichment and extension. At the same time, the program must recognise that the students have learning disabilities that require help and the development of strategies for overcoming their challenges. Research by Foley Nicpon, Allman, Sieck and Stinson (2011) found that a number of students who are academically gifted with learning disabilities have not received appropriate educational services.

Preassessment

Preassessment is great, if a teacher takes it on board. Once a teacher recognises the diversity among their students from the preassessment, they must then adjust their objectives and instructional techniques. Being flexible in what a teacher wants their students to accomplish also requires flexibility with their resources. It is important that teachers allow students to use whatever media is appropriate to their learning and expression styles and the teachers instructional goals. The following questionnaires will help give treachers more insight into their 2e students.

Questions for students

- Tell me about school and what you like and dislike about it.
- What do you find easy to do, difficult to do?
- Describe your ideal teacher/school/classroom.
- What do you do outside school?
- Can you give me an analogy of how you feel about yourself?
- If you had the option to have input into work undertaken in the classroom and assignments set for you, what sort of things would you tell the teacher you would like?

Questions for parents

- Tell me about your child.
- When was your child first identified as gifted with a learning disability?
- Who identified the disability or giftedness?
- How was your child identified as gifted with a learning disability?
- What strategies have you implemented to support your child?
- Has the school/ teachers addressed the issues your child has at school, with school work, and how have they done this?
- What has been the effect on the family?

Questions for teachers

- Tell me about Scott. What was he like in the classroom?
- How did you identify that he was gifted when other teachers had targeted him as only having a disability?
- Why did you advocate for Scott and request that he be allowed to attend the school for longer than the usual designated time?

2e FACT SHEET

WHAT DOES IT MEAN TO BE TWICE-EXCEPTIONAL (2e)?

2e students have exceptional talents while also experiencing learning disabilities such as ADHD, autism, and dyslexia. They often have deep passions and strengths and shine in those areas, but are sometimes seen as lazy or obstinate outside of their interests.

2e IDENTIFICATION MATTERS!

Even if they perform at grade level, 2e students are overtaxed using their gifts to compensate for their disability, or underperform if their disability masks their gifts.

2e students develop asynchronously. For example, a 4th grader may:
- Understand math at a 7th grade level
- Write at a 2nd grade level
- Socialize at a 1st grade level
- Reason at a 12th grade level

Developmental asynchrony often results in anxiety and depression; students may feel deficient despite having incredible intellectual and creative strengths. When combined with sensory overstimulaton and impulse control issues, children may experience behavioral challenges in the classroom.

With proper support, 2e students can reach their potential, shine in their classrooms, and become amazing future contributors to society.

WHAT THEY FEEL

MISUNDERSTOOD
TEASED PRESSURED DIFFERENT
UNDERVALUED LONELY ANXIOUS
DEPRESSED NOT GOOD ENOUGH
OVER/UNDER STIMULATED
PRETENDING TO BE "NORMAL"

WHAT YOU SEE

Acting impulsively, acting out
Attempting to escape tasks
Pacing, fidgeting, doodling
Looking away, distracted
Trying to self-regulate
Wandering by themselves
Blurting out answers
Shutting down

Top tips for working with 2e kids

LET THEIR STRENGTHS SHINE
Ask children and parents to identify strengths and interests, then build on these to unlock their potential.

BE CURIOUS AND EMPATHETIC
There is always a logic to frustrating behavior. 2e kids don't intend to give teachers a hard tme, rather they are having a hard tme.

ADJUST LEVEL TO ASYNCHRONOUS DEVELOPMENT
Even though 2e children are bright, they cannot master every subject at the same level or pace.

COLLABORATE WITH THEIR TEAM
Ask parents, previous teachers, and their psychologists, behaviorists, etc. to learn what works.

Changemakers

Anthony Hopkins
Distinguished Actor
AUTISM

Octavia Butler
Prescient Author
DYSLEXIA

Simone Biles
Olympic Gymnast
ADHD

learn more at reel2e.org

THANKS REEL. HTTPS://WWW.REEL2E.ORG

Gifted Children's
Bill of Rights

You have a right . . .

. . . to know about your giftedness.

. . . to learn something new every day.

. . . to be passionate about your talent area without apologies.

. . . to have an identity beyond your talent area.

. . . to feel good about your accomplishments.

. . . to make mistakes.

. . . to seek guidance in the development of your talent.

. . . to have multiple peer groups and a variety of friends.

. . . to choose which of your talent areas you wish to pursue.

. . . not to be gifted at everything.

—Del Siegle
2007–2009 NAGC President

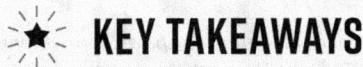

KEY TAKEAWAYS

- **Role of technology and AI:** Technology, including AI tools like ChatGPT, can provide valuable support for 2e students when used appropriately. However, it's essential to understand both the benefits and limitations of these tools, and to provide clear guidelines for their utilisation in educational settings.

- **Classroom accommodations and modifications:** Successful support for 2e students requires a range of accommodations, from extended time on assessments to assistive technologies. These modifications should be tailored to individual students' needs whilst building on their strengths and interests.

- **Assessment and information gathering:** Pre-assessment and ongoing evaluation are crucial for understanding 2e students' needs. Utilising structured questionnaires for students, parents, and teachers helps build a comprehensive picture of the student's strengths, challenges, and learning preferences.

- **Differentiated programme delivery:** Effective teaching for 2e students requires differentiation in content, process, and product. This includes providing multiple ways for students to access information, engage with material, and demonstrate their understanding.

- **Importance of student choice:** Offering students choice in their learning activities and assessment methods is essential for engagement and success. This approach helps accommodate their unique learning styles whilst building on their strengths and interests.

Chapter references

Baum, S., Schader, R., & Owens, V. (2017). *To be gifted and learning disabled: Strength-based strategies for helping twice-exceptional students* (3rd ed.). Prufrock Press.

Baum, S., Novak, C., Preuss, L., & Dann, M. (2009). Twice-exceptional learners: Understanding and meeting their needs. *2e Newsletter, 36*, 17–22.

Bowler, J. (2023). *Study with me: Effective tools and strategies for active learning*. Penguin Books.

Eide, B. L., & Eide, F. F. (2023). *The dyslexic advantage: Unlocking the hidden potential of the dyslexic brain* (Updated ed.). Plume.

Eide, B., & Eide, F. F. (2006). *The mislabeled child*. Hyperion.

Foley Nicpon, M., Allman, A., Sieck, B., & Stinson, R. D. (2011). Empirical investigation of twice-exceptionality: Where have we been and where are we going? *Gifted Child Quarterly, 55*(1), 3–17.

Foss, B. (2013). *The dyslexia empowerment plan*. Ballantine Books.

Leppien, J. H., & Thomas, T. M. (2016). Revealing the strengths of 2e students by using technology. *Teaching Exceptional Children, 48*(4), 76–85.

Maker, C. J. (1982). *Curriculum development for the gifted*. Pro-Ed.

Tomlinson, C. A. (2017). *How to differentiate instruction in academically diverse classrooms* (3rd ed.). ASCD.

CHAPTER 13

The Continuum of Empowerment: Sustaining 2e Support

Dr Christine Ireland

Planting seeds of awareness

The journey of sustaining 2e support begins with awareness. In this chapter we will discuss strategies for raising awareness among fellow educators, professionals, families, and the broader community. By shedding light on the intricacies of twice exceptionality, you'll contribute to a more inclusive and informed educational landscape.

Navigating the educational landscape for 2e learners can be a daunting and complex journey, marked by a lack of unified approaches to support and accommodate their diverse needs. While these students possess exceptional gifts alongside neurodiversity or learning challenges, the educational system often struggles to provide comprehensive and tailored support to help them thrive. Across Australia, numerous support agencies and organisations strive to assist families with children requiring additional support. These organisations offer a wide range of services, including advocacy, information dissemination, counselling, and educational resources, to empower families and ensure that 2e learners receive the support they need to reach their full potential.

Some prominent support agencies in Australia include:

- The Gifted Support Network (GSN) – https://www.giftedsupport.org/
- Autism Spectrum Australia (Aspect) – https://www.autismspectrum.org.au/
- ADHD Australia – https://www.adhdaustralia.org.au/
- Deaf Children Australia – https://deafchildrenaustralia.org.au/
- The Cerebral Palsy Alliance – https://www.cpaustralia.com.au/
- The Australian Association of Special Education – https://aase.edu.au/
- Down Syndrome Australia – https://www.downsyndrome.org.au/
- The Raising Children Network – https://raisingchildren.net.au/

These organisations play a crucial role in supporting teachers and families, raising awareness, and advocating for inclusive and equitable education for 2e learners across Australia. By leveraging their expertise and resources, families can access valuable support networks and services to navigate the complexities of supporting their children's unique needs within the educational system.

Professional development and lifelong learning

As the field of education evolves, so too do the opportunities for professional development. However, Australian teachers are typically not required to complete post-graduate training in gifted education. According to research by Ireland, Bowles, Nikakis, and Brindle (2020), undergraduate training in gifted education in Australia is minimal, leaving many educators underprepared to meet the needs of gifted and 2e students. Appropriate professional development in this area could significantly improve the extension opportunities provided for highly able students, especially those with twice-exceptionalities.

The Senate Review (2001) on Gifted Children highlighted the need for better teacher training and curriculum support, stating, "Better training and better curriculum support are essential to ensure that teachers are able to differentiate the curriculum for gifted students" (p. viii). Watters (2013) further illustrated how professional learning might look through a long-term initiative offered to 56 teachers over eight years. In this program, teachers were encouraged to take an active role in shaping their professional development by using an action research framework to design, implement, and reflect on projects that expanded over a three-year period. This approach allowed educators to engage deeply with gifted education, progressively building their capacity to meet the needs of highly able and twice-exceptional students.

Watters' research underscores the importance of ongoing, tailored professional development, a point echoed by Ireland et al. (2020), who demonstrated that professional learning for gifted students must be continuous. In their study, all 27 surveyed teachers agreed that gifted and highly able students required special attention, and the majority felt that schools were responsible for providing this support. However, many teachers expressed concerns about the potential for 'labelling' students in special programs and were hesitant about practices like grade-skipping. These attitudes suggest that further professional development and research into best practices for gifted and twice-exceptional education would be beneficial to help address such concerns and improve teacher preparedness.

To enhance professional development for educators working with gifted and 2e students, several resources are available. The Gifted Education Research, Resource and Information Centre (GERRIC) at the University of New South Wales provides workshops, courses, and conferences aimed at helping educators better understand and support gifted learners. Similarly, organisations such as the Australian Association for the Education of the Gifted and Talented (AAEGT) and its state affiliates, including the Victorian Association for Gifted and Talented Children (VGATC), offer professional development through conferences, seminars, and online resources. Additionally, platforms like the Australian Council for Educational Research (ACER) offer courses and webinars specifically designed to meet the needs of diverse learners, including gifted and 2e students. By engaging with these resources, educators can enhance their pedagogical practices and better meet the needs of gifted and twice-exceptional students in their classrooms, ensuring that these learners receive the support they need to thrive academically and emotionally.

The data in the following diagram (from C. H. Ireland. University of Melbourne, Doctor of Education, September 2022) are also applicable to 2e students.

Figure 1: Teachers' Perceptions of Issues Relating to Provision of Extension for Highly Able Students

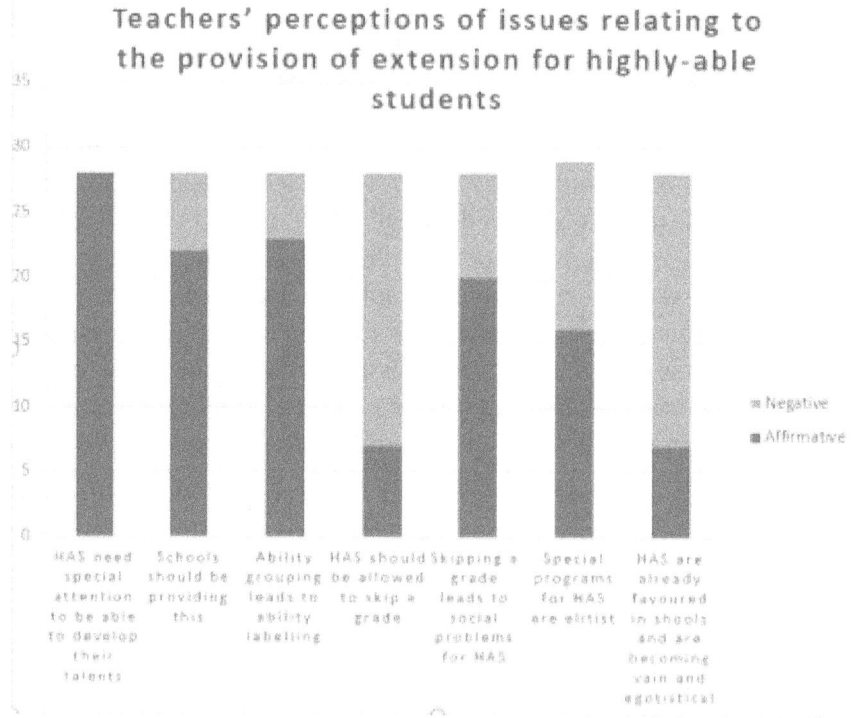

Creating sustainable support systems

Sustaining support for 2e learners requires more than just individual efforts; it necessitates the creation of comprehensive systems within educational institutions. One effective strategy is to embed 2e education principles within the policies, practices, and culture of the school. This involves integrating accommodations, resources, and ongoing training for educators that specifically address the needs of 2e learners. By institutionalising support, schools ensure that their commitment to 2e education extends beyond individual efforts, creating a consistent and enduring framework. Teachers play a key role in advocating for such systems, ensuring that the unique needs of 2e students are recognised and addressed across all levels of the institution.

Incorporating 2e education principles into school policies requires a revision of existing guidelines to explicitly consider the needs of 2e learners. This includes advocating for the development of policies around identification and assessment procedures, individualised education plans (IEPs), and appropriate classroom accommodations. Institutions should also establish professional development programs to help educators understand and support 2e students more effectively. By formalising these practices, schools signal their commitment to equitable opportunities for all learners, including those who are both gifted and challenged (Cross & Cross, 2015). Such a structured approach not only benefits 2e students but also fosters a more inclusive and adaptable learning environment for the entire school community.

Parents play a critical role in this institutionalisation process. By advocating for their child, they can push for changes that benefit all 2e learners. Parental advocacy often involves encouraging schools to upskill staff, reminding them of inclusive language and practice, and advocating for ongoing professional development. Parents are the driving force behind ensuring that schools recognise the importance of creating a lasting framework of support. By working together with educators, parents can ensure that their child's educational needs are met and that a system is in place to support future 2e learners (Pfeiffer, 2018).

A robust support network is equally vital for parents of gifted or 2e children. Studies highlight the importance of parental involvement in improving the wellbeing and academic outcomes of 2e learners (Cross & Cross, 2015). Engaging with other parents who are facing similar challenges fosters mutual understanding and provides access to resources and shared experiences (Mofield & Peters-Burton, 2020). Such networks offer emotional support and practical advice, enabling parents to navigate the complex educational landscape with greater confidence and effectiveness. Through these collaborations, parents become more empowered advocates, working alongside schools to create the best possible educational environment for their child.

The list below is not an exhaustiv. It considers local and social media groups that encourage support and advocacy. As a parent, you are not alone, and you do not need to reinvent the wheel. The following support networks have access to resources and evidence to strengthen your position when you talk to your child's learning institution:

- Twice Exceptional Children's Advocacy (TECA) – https://www.teca2e.org/

- Supporting the Emotional Needs of the Gifted (SENG) – https://www.sengifted.org/
- Gifted and Talented Children's Association of South Australia (GTCASA) – https://gtcasa.asn.au/
- Gifted Families Support Group Inc. (GFSG) – https://www.giftedfamilies.org.au/
- Autism Spectrum Australia (Aspect) – https://www.autismspectrum.org.au/
- ADHD Australia – https://www.adhdaustralia.org.au/
- Raising Children Network – https://raisingchildren.net.au/
- Deaf Children Australia – https://deafchildrenaustralia.org.au/

Australia's Disability Strategy 2021–31 outlines a ten-year vision to enhance the lives of individuals with disabilities, with one key outcome area focused on education and learning. A significant priority within this strategy is improving pathways and accessibility to further education and training for students with disabilities. However, despite the strategy's ambition, it currently lacks a mechanism to involve student voice, particularly the voices of twice-exceptional (2e) students, in policy development. This gap contrasts with international efforts, such as Denmark's annual wellbeing surveys for public schoolchildren. Since 2014, Denmark has implemented a 40-question survey for students in grades 4–9, focusing on social wellbeing. These results are not only shared with the government and stakeholders but also used to monitor and address issues, like the correlation between student wellbeing and parental disadvantage, leading to informed improvements in public schools.

Australia's education system could become a global leader by addressing the complex needs of 2e students, offering simultaneous support and extension within mainstream classrooms, while engaging the entire education community in these efforts. Addressing both the disabilities and the gifts of these students requires a dual approach that is often overlooked. Currently, Australia's Federal and State Education Departments must take a more proactive stance in supporting 2e students, ensuring their right to a meaningful and challenging education that develops their capabilities.

As Teather and Hillman (2017) noted, 133,000 Australian students with disabilities are either receiving inadequate support or no special arrangements in schools. Among these students are 2e learners, whose complex profiles often go unnoticed or unmet within traditional classroom settings. These students require tailored learning environments that address both their need for support in specific areas of weakness, and opportunities for extension in areas of strength. Providing a range of educational options, such as targeted Individual Learning Plans (ILPs) and access to specialised resources, can significantly boost both educational achievement and student satisfaction, ensuring that all students, including those who are 2e, are able to reach their full potential.

Amplifying student voice

Twice-exceptional learners possess a unique blend of exceptional abilities and learning challenges, often requiring specialised support to thrive in educational settings. However, viewing them solely as recipients of support overlooks their potential as agents of change within the education system. Empower 2e learners to become advocates for their own needs, express their perspectives, and influence educational decisions. By amplifying their voices, we can create a more inclusive and effective learning environment that benefits all students.

To empower 2e learners, it is essential to understand their experiences and challenges. 2e students often face a myriad of obstacles, including navigating conflicting identities, managing asynchronous development, and coping with societal misconceptions about giftedness and disabilities. According to Silverman (2013), 2e individuals may struggle with a sense of belonging and may feel misunderstood or overlooked in traditional educational settings. By recognising the complexity of the 2e experience, educators and policymakers can better support these learners in achieving their full potential.

Empowering 2e learners begins with amplifying their voices and providing opportunities for self-advocacy. Research by Robinson and Noble (2019) emphasises the importance of giving 2e students a platform to express their perspectives, share their challenges, and contribute to discussions about their educational needs. This can be achieved through student-led initiatives, such as peer support groups, student councils, and involvement in decision-making processes at both the classroom and institutional levels. By actively listening to 2e students and valuing their input, educators can foster a sense of agency and empowerment.

In addition to providing opportunities for self-expression, educators play a crucial role in equipping 2e learners with the skills they need to advocate for themselves effectively. According to Moon and Reis (2020), self-advocacy skills include self-awareness, communication, problem-solving, and resilience. Educators can integrate self-advocacy instruction into the curriculum, teaching students how to identify their strengths and challenges, articulate their needs, and seek out appropriate support when necessary. By empowering 2e students to advocate for themselves, educators foster independence and self-efficacy, essential qualities for success in school and beyond.

Empowering 2e learners to become agents of change also involves their participation in educational decision-making processes. Research by Gallagher and Johnson (2018) highlights the benefits of including student voice in policy development, program planning, and curriculum design. By inviting 2e students to participate in discussions about their educational experiences, educators and policymakers gain valuable insights into the effectiveness of existing support systems and areas for improvement. This collaborative approach ensures that educational decisions are informed by the perspectives and needs of those directly affected by them, leading to more responsive and inclusive practices.

Passing the torch: Legacy of empowerment

In closing this chapter, we will reflect on the legacy some educators and families are creating as they sustain 2e support. Just as these stakeholder have been inspired by the journey, they too have the power to inspire others including fellow educators, professionals, families, and future generations. Their commitment to sustaining empowerment ensures that the spark they have ignited continues to light the way.

As stakeholders step forward into the continuum of empowerment, remember that the path that has been forged is not just a chapter in a book; it's a lifelong commitment to nurturing exceptional minds, fostering growth, and celebrating the unique potential of every 2e learner. This ongoing dedication shapes the future of education itself.

★ KEY TAKEAWAYS

- **Awareness as the foundation:** Raising awareness about twice exceptionality among educators, families, and communities is critical to fostering a more inclusive educational landscape. Highlighting the unique challenges and strengths of 2e learners helps combat misconceptions and drive meaningful change.

- **The role of professional development:** Many educators lack sufficient training in gifted education and 2e student support. Comprehensive, ongoing professional development opportunities, such as action research frameworks and workshops provided by organisations like GERRIC, are essential to equipping teachers with the tools they need.

- **Sustainable systems:** Embedding 2e education principles into school policies ensures consistent, long-term support. This includes developing Individual Learning Plans (ILPs), advocating for tailored assessments, and establishing a culture of inclusive practices across institutions.

- **Amplifying student voice:** Empowering 2e learners to advocate for their own needs and participate in educational decision-making fosters independence, resilience, and a sense of belonging. Educators can integrate self-advocacy instruction to help students articulate their needs and strengths effectively.

- **Collaborative advocacy:** Parents and educators must work together to institutionalise 2e support systems. Advocacy by parents and collaboration within support networks are vital for ensuring that educational institutions prioritise the needs of 2e learners while leveraging available resources.

Chapter references

Cross, T. L., & Cross, J. R. (2015). *Handbook for Counselors Serving Students with Gifts and Talents: Development, Relationships, School Issues, and Counseling Needs/Interventions.* Prufrock Press.

Ireland, C. H., Bowles, T., Nikakis, C., & Brindle, K. (2020). Educators' perceptions of professional development in gifted education. *The Australasian Journal of Gifted Education, 29*(1), 21–34.

Gallagher, J. J., & Johnson, A. (2018). The role of student voice in gifted education policy and practice. *Journal for the Education of the Gifted, 41*(4), 402–419.

Mofield, E., & Peters-Burton, E. (2020). Supporting twice-exceptional learners: Strategies for bridging the divide. *Teaching Exceptional Children, 52*(4), 216–227.

Moon, S. M., & Reis, S. M. (2020). Self-advocacy and twice-exceptional students. *Gifted Child Today, 43*(1), 10–17.

Pfeiffer, S. I. (2018). *Essentials of Gifted Assessment.* Wiley.

Robinson, A., & Noble, T. (2019). Advocating for the voices of gifted and twice-exceptional students. *Gifted Education International, 35*(3), 194–210.

Silverman, L. K. (2013). *Giftedness 101.* Springer Publishing Company.

Senate Employment, Workplace Relations, Small Business and Education References Committee. (2001). *The education of gifted children.* Commonwealth of Australia.

Teather, S., & Hillman, S. (2017). Supporting students with disabilities in Australian schools: Equity, inclusion, and the current state of play. *Educational Review, 69*(3), 329–345.

Watters, J. J. (2013). Professional learning for teachers of the gifted: Developing expertise through action research. *Australasian Journal of Gifted Education, 22*(2), 42–56.

CHAPTER 14

Continuing the Adventure: A Future of 2e Excellence

Rhiannon Lowrey

As we reach the culmination of our journey into the world of twice-exceptional (2e) education, it's important to pause and reflect on the insights we've gained, the challenges we've addressed, and the progress we've celebrated. Throughout this exploration, we've uncovered the unique needs, strengths, and potential of 2e learners. Your commitment as an educator, advocate, or supporter has underscored the profound impact you have on their lives. The moments of understanding you've gained, the strategies you've implemented, and the successes you've witnessed all contribute to a broader movement towards more inclusive and equitable education. The knowledge you've acquired equips you to continue advocating for 2e learners and to create environments where they can flourish.

Celebrating progress

- The strides made in 2e education are truly worth celebrating. Increased awareness of twice exceptionality, evolving support systems, and more inclusive educational practices have transformed classrooms into spaces that better cater to the needs of diverse learners. Where once the potential of 2e students was overlooked, educators are now recognising that neurodiversity is an asset that contributes to a richer learning environment.

Key progress points include:

- **Differentiated instruction:** Educators have embraced practices that allow for tailored learning experiences, considering the asynchronous development of 2e students.
- **Inclusion policies:** Schools are increasingly implementing Individualised Education Plans (IEPs) and targeted interventions that balance both challenges and strengths.
- **Technological support:** Assistive technologies and AI tools are making it possible for 2e learners to move from dependence to independence, empowering them to demonstrate knowledge in new and creative ways.

These milestones represent a collective effort to transform education into a system where all students, regardless of their neurodiverse profiles, feel valued and supported.

A vision for the future

Looking ahead, we can envision a future where 2e learners are fully embraced as integral contributors to the educational landscape. Imagine classrooms where every teacher is trained to recognise and nurture the unique potential of 2e students. In this vision:

- Strength-based approaches replace deficit-focused interventions.
- Empathy and understanding guide educators in addressing challenges and providing accommodations.
- Collaborative partnerships between families, schools, and external organisations ensure consistent, well-rounded support.

In this future, educational institutions proactively develop policies that recognise the complexity of 2e learners, integrating advanced screening methods, inclusive practices, and professional development into their systems. Schools would not merely accommodate but celebrate these students, providing platforms for their voices and talents to shine.

A neuroaccepting classroom would see a dynamic, inclusive environment where diverse neurocognitive profiles are not only accommodated but celebrated. Such a space prioritises equity, respect, and individuality, creating a safe and stimulating learning environment for all students, including those with twice-exceptional (2e) profiles. Practices could include differentiated instruction tailored to students' unique strengths and challenges, flexible seating options to support sensory and physical needs, and the integration of assistive technologies like speech-to-text tools and AI-driven learning platforms. Social-emotional learning (SEL) would be explicitly taught, providing students with strategies to regulate emotions, build resilience, and foster peer relationships. Supports could include sensory-friendly zones, access to Individualised Education Plans (IEPs), and a collaborative network of educators, families, and specialists. Professional development for teachers would be ongoing, equipping them to recognise and nurture neurodiversity through strength-based approaches. Ultimately, a neuroaccepting classroom would thrive as a community where differences are viewed as assets, and all students are empowered to excel academically, socially, and emotionally.

A neuroaccepting classroom serves as the foundation for cultivating a society that values and harnesses the strengths of neurodiverse individuals, including in the workplace. Just as inclusive educational environments accommodate diverse learning needs, neuroaccepting workplaces can provide accommodations to empower employees and maximise their potential. For example, flexible work arrangements, such as remote work or adjustable hours, can support individuals with ADHD or sensory sensitivities by allowing them to work during their most productive times or in environments suited to their needs. Quiet spaces or sensory-friendly rooms, akin to the sensory zones in classrooms, can help neurodivergent employees manage overstimulation. Assistive technologies, such as speech-to-text software or organisational tools like Trello, can support employees with dyslexia or executive functioning challenges. Neurodiverse hiring initiatives, such as Special Access Programs (SAP), and Microsoft, demonstrate how workplaces can actively recruit and create supportive roles for individuals with autism, leveraging their unique strengths in detail-oriented tasks, pattern recognition, or innovative thinking. Training managers and teams in neurodiversity awareness can foster an inclusive culture, ensuring that colleagues and leaders understand how to collaborate effectively while valuing diverse contributions. By extending the principles of neuroacceptance from classrooms to workplaces, we build a society where differences are embraced, strengths are amplified, and all individuals can contribute meaningfully, no longer feeling othered.

Empowering 2e voices

To achieve this future, we must centre the voices of 2e learners themselves. These students have unique insights into their own needs and can provide invaluable feedback to shape educational policies and practices. By empowering 2e learners as advocates for their education, we move closer to an inclusive framework that reflects their experiences.

Strategies to empower 2e voices include:

1. **Self-advocacy programs:** Teaching students how to articulate their needs, strengths, and preferences equips them to navigate challenges with confidence.
2. **Student representation:** Including 2e learners as representatives on school councils, policy discussions, and curriculum design ensures that their perspectives influence decision-making.
3. **Mentorship opportunities:** Pairing younger 2e students with older peers or role models fosters a sense of belonging and encourages leadership.

By amplifying their voices, we not only elevate 2e learners but also create a culture that values diversity, resilience, and innovation.

Current initiatives aimed at building advocacy and amplifying the voices of twice-exceptional individuals are creating meaningful change in education and beyond. Organisations like **Supporting Emotional Needs of the Gifted (SENG)** and **Twice Exceptional Children's Advocacy (TECA)** provide platforms for 2e individuals, families, and educators to share their experiences, engage in advocacy, and access resources tailored to their needs. **Autism Spectrum Australia (Aspect)** and similar groups host workshops and community forums to empower 2e individuals to speak about their challenges and strengths, fostering self-advocacy skills. Educational programs like the **Gifted Education Research and Resource Information Centre (GERRIC)** at UNSW focus on professional development to better support 2e students; while initiatives such as **Project Uplift** in the United States promote neurodiversity awareness through public speaking opportunities for neurodiverse individuals. Internationally, companies like **Microsoft's Autism Hiring Program** not only provide employment pathways but also amplify the voices of neurodiverse employees by showcasing their contributions. Online platforms, webinars, and podcasts, such as the **Neurodiversity Podcast**, further highlight personal stories of 2e individuals, giving them a global stage to inform and inspire others. These initiatives are instrumental in shifting societal perceptions, creating pathways for inclusion, and empowering 2e individuals to advocate for their needs and shape their futures.

The future of twice-exceptional education

As we consider the road ahead, it's clear that the journey doesn't end here. The insights gained from working with 2e learners reveal pathways to broader educational reform. The principles that benefit 2e students – individualisation, empathy, and creativity – can elevate learning for all students.

Priorities for the future should include:

1. **Teacher training:** Expanding professional development to include 2e education will empower educators with the tools to identify and support these learners effectively. Training should encompass both academic differentiation and social-emotional learning.
2. **Collaboration with families:** Strengthening partnerships between schools and families ensures consistent, well-informed support for 2e learners. Schools must actively engage parents as allies in their child's education.
3. **Policy reform:** Advocating for systemic changes at the local, state, and national levels will ensure that 2e students are recognised and supported within educational frameworks.
4. **Research and innovation:** Continued research into the experiences, needs, and outcomes of 2e learners will provide data-driven insights to guide future practices.
5. **Technological integration:** Harnessing the potential of AI, assistive technologies, and other innovations will help 2e learners overcome challenges and explore their strengths.

A call to action

Educators, policymakers, and advocates must unite to champion the needs of 2e learners. The journey requires ongoing effort, a willingness to embrace change, and a commitment to seeing every student as a complex individual with unique potential.

Your role in the future

As an educator or advocate, your role in shaping the future of 2e education is critical. Every time you adapt a lesson, advocate for a student, or share your knowledge with colleagues, you contribute to a culture of inclusivity. Your dedication to understanding and supporting 2e learners lays the foundation for a future where every student can thrive.

Continuing the adventure

The adventure of twice-exceptional education is one of continuous discovery. The strategies, tools, and insights you've gained are the beginning of a lifelong commitment to growth and advocacy. As you move forward, seek out opportunities to expand your knowledge, share your experiences, and collaborate with others who are passionate about this work. Remember that every small step you take has the potential to create lasting change.

A future of excellence

As we conclude this chapter, reflect on the progress we've made and the potential that lies ahead. By embracing the principles of equity, empathy, and innovation, we can build a future where every 2e learner is empowered to redefine what excellence means. The commitment you've shown to supporting these exceptional minds ensures that this journey will continue – towards a world where every student's potential is celebrated, and no one is left behind.

Thank you for embarking on this journey with us. Together, we are shaping a brighter, more inclusive future for all learners.

 **KEY TAKEAWAYS**

- **Celebrating neurodiversity:** The chapter marks a transformative shift in 2e education, moving from deficit-focused approaches to recognising neurodiversity as a valuable asset. Increased awareness and inclusive practices are creating educational environments that honour the unique potential of twice-exceptional learners.

- **Neuroaccepting environments:** A vision emerges of classrooms and workplaces that go beyond mere accommodation, actively celebrating and supporting neurodivergent individuals. This includes implementing flexible learning strategies, assistive technologies, and policies that recognise the strengths of 2e learners across educational and professional settings.

- **Empowering student voices:** Centring the experiences of 2e learners themselves is crucial. This involves developing robust self-advocacy programs, creating meaningful representation in educational decision-making, and establishing mentorship opportunities that amplify the perspectives of twice-exceptional individuals.

- **Comprehensive support ecosystem:** The future of 2e education demands a holistic approach, integrating ongoing teacher training, collaborative family partnerships, policy reforms, continued research, and technological innovations to create a supportive, adaptive educational landscape.

- **Continuous advocacy and growth:** Supporting 2e learners is presented as an ongoing journey of discovery, requiring persistent commitment, empathy, and innovation. Every small step towards understanding and supporting these learners contributes to a more inclusive future that celebrates individual potential.

www.ingramcontent.com/pod-product-compliance
Lightning Source LLC
Chambersburg PA
CBHW070036140526
PP18295900001B/1